DUST-UP

DUST-UP

Asbestos Litigation and the Failure
of Commonsense Policy Reform

JEB BARNES

Georgetown University Press / Washington, D.C.

Georgetown University Press, Washington, D.C. www.press.georgetown.edu

Library of Congress Cataloging-in-Publication Data

Barnes, Jeb.
  Dust-up : asbestos litigation and the failure of commonsense policy reform / Jeb Barnes.
    p. cm.
  Includes bibliographical references and index.
  ISBN 978-1-58901-766-5 (pbk. : alk. paper)
  1. Products liability—Asbestos—United States.
2. Damages—United States. 3. Asbestos—Law and legislation—United States—History. 4. Law reform—United States. I. Title.
  KF1297.A73B37 2011
  344.04'6335—dc22

                                                    2010041418

♾ This book is printed on acid-free paper meeting the requirements of the American National Standard for Permanence in Paper for Printed Library Materials.

15 14 13 12 11   9 8 7 6 5 4 3 2
First printing

Printed in the United States of America

CONTENTS

ILLUSTRATIONS

Figures

Tables

LIST OF ILLUSTRATIONS

PREFACE

One of my favorite fortune cookies reads: "To teach is to learn twice." This book embodies that aphorism. In 2005 I returned to the University of Southern California from a two-year stint at the University of California, Berkeley, School of Public Health as a Robert Wood Johnson Scholar in Health Policy, an innovative interdisciplinary program that seeks to draw new scholars into the field of health policy research. During my fellowship I studied the policy implications of American reliance on litigation to address public health issues, and I was eager to include this material in my courses on American politics and law and public policy. One of my new lectures focused on the cost and unpredictability of American asbestos litigation relative to the centralized social insurance programs found in other economically advanced democracies. These comparisons repeatedly begged a key question: If asbestos litigation in the United States is so woefully inefficient and unfair, why has Congress repeatedly failed to replace it? This question caused me to revisit what I had learned during my fellowship. The more I looked, the more intrigued I became, because the story of asbestos litigation reform seemed to defy conventional wisdom at every turn.

This volume is the culmination of my inquiry. Given its origins, the main purpose of this project is to teach students about the complexity of the American policymaking process and, along the way, push them to think beyond the specialized accounts of congressional and judicial behavior that dominate media accounts and the academic literature and to consider how policy and politics emanate from interactions among different branches and levels of government. A secondary purpose is to illustrate how case studies, despite their obvious limitations, can advance the research cycle, even from a perspective that ultimately sets its sights on hypothesis testing in large-N, variable-based studies. The hope is that this case study will find a place in seminars on American politics, health policy, and law and public policy and will be used by other teachers to encourage students to think more carefully about the sometimes inspiring, sometimes maddening, always interesting back and forth of contemporary US policymaking.

Many wonderful colleagues and friends helped advance this project, and it is my pleasure to acknowledge my indebtedness to them. At Georgetown University Press, a special debt is owed to Gail Grella, who first expressed interest in this project, to Don Jacobs, Gail's successor, whose endless patience gave it a chance to come to fruition, and to the reviewers, for their penetrating and constructive comments. At Berkeley, Robert A. Kagan and Stephen Sugarman served as my mentors in the Scholars in Health Policy Program and offered tireless advice and insight. Special thanks are due to Patrick Hanlon at Berkeley, to R. Shep Melnick at Boston College, and to Thomas F. Burke at Wellesley College, who offered searching critiques of early drafts that greatly improved the book, and to the interviewees who took time out of their busy schedules and received nothing in return other than the promise of confidentiality. I also owe a deep intellectual debt to Kathleen Thelen at the Massachusetts Institute of Technology, to the participants in the 2006 Institutional Change and Law Workshop at Northwestern University, to Marty Levin at Brandeis University, and to the participants in the 2007 Workshop on Contemporary Governance, whose comments inspired the framing of the analysis and encouraged me to continue to develop the idea of the politics of efficiency. I am equally indebted to two graduate students at the University of Southern California, Jesse Mills and Parker Hevron, whose timely and energetic research assistance was critical in pushing the project to completion. I look forward to reading their books and articles on American politics. Of course, any errors that survived these fine scholars' best efforts at correction remain entirely my own.

Finally, and above all, I thank my loving wife, Annie Barnes, whose partnership, kindness, and intelligence supported every word of this manuscript, and to my two boys, Alexander and Ryan, who provided much-needed breaks for, among other things, football, soccer, baseball, bike riding, ping pong, surfing, swimming, and Lego building.

Part I

Background

CHAPTER 1

Today's Challenging Legislative Environment and the Politics of Efficiency

For some time, I've had a growing conviction that Congress is not operating as it should. There is too much partisanship and not enough progress—too much narrow ideology and not enough practical problem solving. Even at a time of enormous national challenge, the people's business is not getting done.

—SENATOR EVAN BAYH (D-IN), on why he was retiring from the Senate, *Los Angeles Times*, February 16, 2010

On September 9, 2009, President Barack Obama addressed a joint session of Congress on the need for major health care reform. Standing before his fellow elected officials and recent congressional colleagues, Obama declared that the "time for bickering is over" and presented his case for a $900 billion plan that would build on the existing employer-based health care system. In the middle of his speech, after he chided opponents for distorting his plan and insisted that it would not cover illegal immigrants or fund abortions, Republican representative Joe Wilson of South Carolina shouted "You lie" (Connolly and Shear 2009).

Congressional leaders quickly condemned Wilson's behavior. He apologized, and President Obama accepted the apology. Rank-and-file Democrats, however, were not so easily appeased. They called for a formal reprimand, and on September 16, 2009, the House of Representatives passed a "resolution of disapproval" against Wilson on a largely party-line vote (Kane 2009). While the Democrats formally rebuked Wilson, the base of the Republican Party embraced him. He reportedly became a minor celebrity among conservatives and "fund-raising star," receiving thousands in campaign contributions, garnering invitations from Republican candidates across the nation, and posing for photographs with the party faithful for $150 (Associated Press 2009).

It is tempting to dismiss this entire episode as overblown and short-lived, a nice moment of drama for the media that quickly passed as new events grabbed the headlines. But Representative Wilson's outburst and its divisive aftermath were not an isolated event. They are emblematic of the sharply partisan landscape in Washington, which reflects several recurring attributes of contemporary politics—namely, the emergence of narrow political majorities and ideologically polarized parties in Congress.

The evidence of shrinking majorities in Congress is striking, especially when placed in historical context. During the nineteenth century, the average margin of congressional control—the difference between the majority and minority parties relative to the total number of seats—was 27.4 percent (Young 2006). In the post–World War II era, the average margin of congressional control fell nearly in half, to 14.3 percent, but healthy majorities were still common. From 1955 to 1993 Democrats held more than 60 percent of House seats in eight of twenty congressional sessions and more than sixty seats in the Senate seven times, and they nearly reached these thresholds in another six sessions, four in the House and two in the Senate.[1]

Things changed with Newt Gingrich's "Contract with America" in 1994. From 1994 to 2009 the margin of party control plummeted to 5.4 percent in the House and 5.2 percent in the Senate (Young 2006). During this period Democrats had more than 60 percent of House seats and sixty Senate seats only once in eight sessions. Moreover, this supermajority in the Senate, which emerged after the election of President Obama in 2008, was tenuous. It included sixty votes only if one counts the two Democratic-leaning independents and only because a Republican senator, Arlen Specter of Pennsylvania, switched parties while making it clear that he would not be an automatic Democratic vote. It was also fleeting. Before the 2010 midterm elections swept the Democratic Party's majority out of the House and significantly reduced the party's majority in the Senate, Republican senator Scott Brown of Massachusetts wrested the critical sixtieth seat from the Democrats in a special election after Senator Edward Kennedy's death (largely by running against the incumbent Democratic majority and President Obama's efforts to pass comprehensive health care legislation).

Under these conditions, the majority party typically cannot unilaterally advance its policy agenda at the federal level, even when it nominally controls Congress and the presidency. Supermajority requirements in the Senate, such as the need for sixty votes to overcome a filibuster, require party leaders to reach across the aisle and muster at least some support from the opposing party.[2] This is especially true today, because the use of the filibuster has reached unprecedented levels. According to the Senate's own data, the filing of motions for cloture—the procedural mechanism for ending filibusters—has grown dramatically during the past fifty years. From 1949 to 1960 a total of 4 cloture motions were filed; but from 1999 to 2010 a total of 547 cloture motions were filed, 136 in the 111th Congress alone (fig. 1.1). These numbers understate the practical importance of supermajority requirements in the contemporary lawmaking process because they do not include other procedural mechanisms that impose sixty-vote thresholds, such as budgetary points of order,[3] or account for how the threat of these obstacles looms over legislative efforts.[4]

Reaching out to members of the minority party, however, creates a political quandary. Efforts to appeal to members of the opposition threaten to alienate the majority party's rank and file, whose loyalty is equally essential to building winning legislative coalitions. This balancing act has become increasingly precarious as ideological tension within Congress has grown over time (see, e.g., Rohde 1991; Aldrich 1995; Groseclose, Levitt, and Snyder 1999; Sinclair 2000a; Roberts and Smith 2003; Jacobson 2007; Poole and Rosenthal 2007). According to Poole and Rosenthal (2007), who have developed widely accepted ideological scores for each member based on an analysis of roll call votes, the distance between the median voter in the Republican and Democratic parties has doubled since the 1980s. Equally important, the distribution among members has shifted. Whereas members were once somewhat evenly distributed across the ideological spectrum, they now tend to cluster at the poles, with Republicans grouped on the right and Democrats clumped on the left.[5]

The point is not that passing major legislation is impossible in an age of polarized and closely divided political parties (Mayhew 2005; Sinclair 2000b). There have been many examples of legislative success on highly contentious issues since 1994, such as the enactment of extensive welfare reform under the Bill Clinton administration, the creation of an expansive prescription drug benefit under the George W. Bush administration, and the passage of the massive fiscal stimulus package, national health care legislation, and sweeping financial reforms under the Obama administration. The point is that the combination of narrow majorities, polarized parties, and supermajority requirements in the Senate creates distinct political challenges (Binder 1998), which often necessitate "unorthodox lawmaking" (Sinclair 2000b). Thus, for example, senators can try to enact a bill using the budget reconciliation process that limits floor debate in both

Figure 1.1. Senate Action on Cloture Motions for Ending Filibusters, 81st to 111th Congresses, 1949–2010

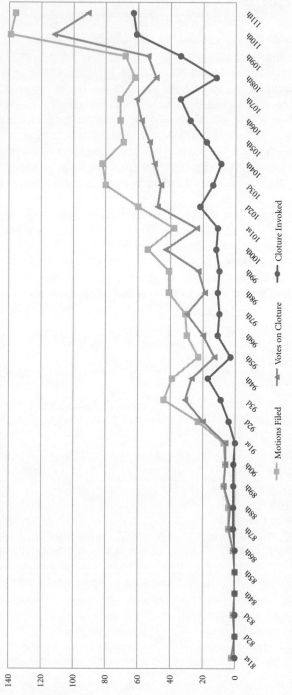

Source: Compiled by the author from data on the US Senate website (www.senate.gov).

chambers and precludes filibusters.[6] Or they can try to build coalitions that avoid straight party-line votes and are broad enough to overcome supermajority requirements in the Senate and/or divided government.

One such coalition-building strategy involves the "politics of efficiency," which frames reforms in terms of their potential to improve the overall efficiency of existing policies and institutional arrangements. The politics of efficiency can potentially diffuse partisan tensions because there are no obvious ideological divisions over making policies and institutions run more smoothly; therefore, the goal of enhancing efficiency seems a valence issue with broad cross-party appeal (see, generally, Esterling 2004; Burke 2002). Consistent with this logic, reformers have called on the politics of efficiency (in some form) since at least the Progressive Era, when advocates promoted their agenda over the opposition of entrenched political parties on the grounds that creating better and more efficient government programs and services was neither inherently Republican nor Democratic. It was merely "good government." The politics of efficiency was also used throughout the 1980s and 1990s to build support for free trade policy, deregulation, and tort reform, as reformers contended that creating the conditions for greater competition and freer markets—such as lower trade barriers, fewer rules, and less litigation—would engender greater efficiency for the benefit of both consumers and producers (Derthick and Quirk 1985).

The politics of efficiency may be particularly salient in coming years given the looming fiscal crisis in the United States. The government reports that the annual federal deficit has more than doubled since 2000 and will reach $1.3 trillion in fiscal year 2011, or about 10 percent of the nation's gross domestic product, while the cumulative debt is projected to hit nearly 95 percent of the gross domestic product, up from 36 percent in 1970 (fig. 1.2). The public has begun to take notice, for it has ranked deficit reduction as a top priority, placing it above health care and education (*Rasmussen Reports* 2009, 2010). The appeal of the politics of efficiency under these conditions is simple. Whereas reducing deficits by raising taxes or retrenching programs is highly partisan and contentious (see, generally, Pierson 1994), squeezing waste out of existing policies and institutions promises to reduce costs without cutting benefits. As such, the politics of efficiency offers something for nothing, which should entice policy entrepreneurs in both political parties.

Of course, theory is one thing; practice is quite another. This book explores the politics of efficiency in the case of the asbestos litigation reform following the 2004 presidential election during the 109th Congress. For

Figure 1.2. Gross Federal Debt as a Percentage of GDP, 1970–2010

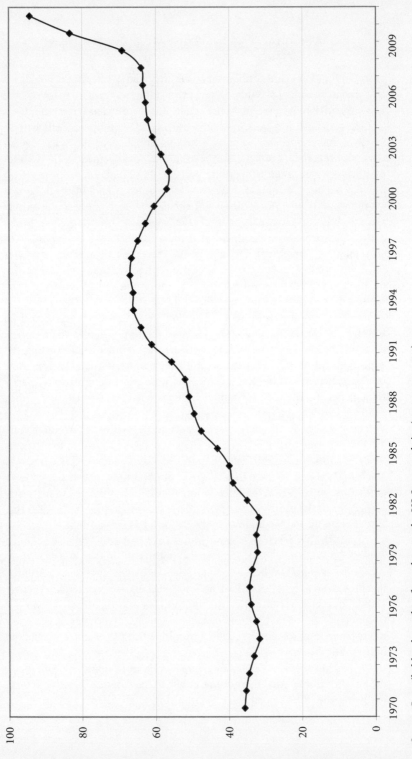

Source: Compiled by the author from data on the US Senate website (www.senate.gov).

reasons discussed below and elaborated in later chapters, this case offers a useful window through which to view the politics of efficiency in action. The main reason is that efficiency arguments were central to promoting asbestos litigation reform in the 109th Congress. Indeed, the politics of efficiency has been at the center of asbestos injury compensation issues since the early 1980s, when advocates for reform both in and outside Washington framed the need for legislative action in terms of the effectiveness and efficiency of litigation as a means of addressing the asbestos crisis. In addition, the politics of efficiency seemed promising for building a winning bipartisan reform coalition in the 109th Congress for a host of political and policy reasons, including the fact that reform promised to deliver billions of dollars in savings to claimant and business interests. Yet no such coalition emerged, and the reform legislation failed.

The question is, Why? Why did the politics of efficiency fail to produce an effective legislative coalition for reforming a system that nearly everyone—the president, congressional leaders, the Supreme Court, and prominent policy analysts—agrees is wasteful, inconsistent, and, in some cases, fraudulent? What does this failure teach us about the promise and limits of the politics of efficiency as a coalition-building strategy and, more generally, the prospects for significant institutional change in today's challenging legislative environment?

THE PUZZLE: A CLOSER LOOK

Exploring the recent politics of asbestos injury compensation takes the analysis into largely uncharted territory. A superb literature documents the cost and inconsistency of asbestos litigation and describes the pertinent judicial decisions and litigation strategies used by lawyers and judges during the past thirty years (e.g., Kakalik et al. 1983; Hensler et al. 1985; Sugarman 1989; McGovern 1989; Hensler et al. 2001; Hensler 2002; Issacharoff 2002; Carroll et al. 2002, 2005; White 2002, 2005; Carrington 2007; Hanlon and Smetak 2007; and see, generally, Nagareda 2007). A smaller body of prescriptive work debates what Congress should do in response to the asbestos crisis (e.g., Glass 1983; Cardozo Symposium 1992; Schwartz, Behrens, and Tedesco 2003; McGovern 2003).

Almost no scholarly attention, however, has been paid to the politics of asbestos injury compensation. Instead, there are several journalistic accounts. Some of these accounts are now dated (Brodeur 1986), and others focus mainly on Libby, Montana—the home of a vermiculite mine that caused this once-pristine town to be designated a toxic waste site (Bowker 2003; Peacock 2003; Schneider and McCumber 2004). To the extent that these accounts touch on the broader politics of asbestos injury compensation, they are impressionistic, providing interesting nuggets of information but no sustained analysis.

Looking beyond the specific literature on the asbestos problem, there is a general literature on the politics of civil litigation in the United States (e.g., O'Connell 1979; Epstein 1988; Elliott and Talarico 1991; Campbell, Kessler, and Shepherd 1995; Kagan 1994, 2001; Barnes 1997; Burke 2002). But the failure of the politics of efficiency in the case of asbestos litigation reform is more, not less, puzzling in light of this body of work. As is more fully described in chapter 3, this literature provides a laundry list of factors that should increase the chances of successfully using the politics of efficiency to build a coalition that can overcome the expected opposition from trial lawyers and pass some type of reform: (1) support from strategically placed policy entrepreneurs, (2) Republican majorities, (3) bipartisan support, (4) judicial calls for legislation, (5) high administrative costs and legal uncertainty, and (6) an expert consensus on the lack of secondary policy benefits of litigation. All these factors were present during the 109th Congress, but the politics of efficiency still failed to create a sufficiently broad bipartisan coalition to push reform across the finish line.

The questions remain: Why did the politics of efficiency fail, given these seemingly favorable political and policy circumstances? Why did stakeholders other than lawyers fail to unite behind reforms that aimed at replacing a notoriously inefficient, inconsistent, and sometimes fraudulent system of compensation that was costing them billions of dollars? What are the broader lessons of this failure?

OVERVIEW OF THE ARGUMENT

This book examines these questions by drawing on multiple sources, including the legislative record, judicial decisions, media accounts, and participant interviews, and by employing multiple methods, including qualitative and quantitative analyses. It aims to describe the recent politics of a major, ongoing public health crisis and to use this substantively important case as a lens to examine the promise and limits of the politics of efficiency. In exploring this issue the book takes up a host of others, including the scope and nature of civil litigation reform, the US system's current capacity for institutional change, and how scholars should grapple with the complexity of contemporary American policymaking.

It needs to be stressed at the outset that this is not a work of pure policy or legal history. No effort is made to provide a comprehensive chronology of recent events in the area of asbestos injury compensation or a detailed examination of the many important legal developments within asbestos litigation. Instead, this book offers a critical case study that aims to identify patterns of interbranch governmental relations that help reveal institutional constraints on improving public policy and the operation of the US legal system for the benefit of both ordinary Americans and businesses. (Appendix A further explains the relevant case study methods, including both their strengths and weaknesses.)

The analysis proceeds in five chapters, which have been divided analytically into three parts: background, case study, and implications. The present chapter has given some of this background, and chapter 2 provides the rest. It offers an overview of the asbestos crisis in the United States by tracing the rise of asbestos consumption and litigation, the growing critiques of asbestos litigation and the related rise of the politics of efficiency, and the institutional response leading up to the latest congressional efforts to reform the system. It argues that the asbestos crisis is best understood as a multifaceted problem that encompasses both a global health crisis and a national institutional crisis, which reflects a deeply layered approach to compensating asbestos victims.

With a better understanding of the underlying policy problem in place, the analysis turns to part II, the case study. Chapter 3 introduces the case by explaining why recent efforts to enact major asbestos injury compensation reform provide a theoretically interesting vantage for exploring the politics of efficiency as a legislative strategy. Chapter 4 provides the heart of the empirical analysis. Drawing on participant interviews and the legislative record as well as analyses of roll call votes and media content, it examines the rise and fall of asbestos litigation reform following the 2004 elections and takes a closer look at why the stakeholders that seemed to have strong incentives to join together remained divided over reforms aimed at reducing costs and improving efficiency.

Part III explores the lessons of the case study in two chapters. Chapter 5 considers the case's implications for the effectiveness of the politics of efficiency as a coalition-building strategy for overcoming party polarization in Congress. On the plus side, the politics of efficiency helped build a broad, bipartisan coalition that came within one vote of overcoming the Senate's supermajority procedural obstacles for highly contentious policy issues. This is not an insignificant achievement, and it shows that the politics of efficiency can engender significant (if not always sufficient) bipartisan support, despite the rancorous atmosphere on Capitol Hill.

Yet the politics of efficiency came up short in the case of asbestos, which, it is contended, suggests two lessons about its limits in today's political environment, especially as applied to civil litigation reform. First, the politics of efficiency emphasizes the *collective* benefits of reducing systemic costs and risks, and thereby it overlooks how litigation shapes the "political economy of civil litigation," the ways in which litigation affects the interests of *individual* stakeholders by determining who pays, how much, and to whom (Epstein 1988; Barnes 2007a). The argument here is that, similar to other types of regulation (Leone 1986; Melnick 1998), litigation distributes costs and risks unevenly. In the case of asbestos this "lumpy" distribution of costs and risks produced a patchwork of winners and losers on the ground, as some business faced high litigation costs while others did not because they had better legal defenses and better insurance coverage or simply were bigger or more profitable and thus were better able to brace against a sudden influx of lawsuits. Similarly, some victims won enormous judgments in the courts while others received nothing. These retail political dynamics undermined the wholesale policy benefits of change by making it harder to find common ground within and among these groups. Without unified support from key stakeholders, asbestos litigation reform legislation faced long odds in the notoriously fractured and cumbersome legislative process in Congress, regardless of its potential to replace a demonstrably costly, unpredictable, and unfair system of compensation.

Second, the case of asbestos illustrates how the "politics of wait and see"—the tendency of Congress to defer controversial issues to other actors—can be the enemy of the politics of efficiency. The politics of wait and see stems from elected officials' natural concern with reelection, which creates strong political incentives to avoid potentially unpopular choices among competing interests. By deferring such issues to the courts, members of Congress can have their cake and eat it, too—they can sidestep tough decisions that might backfire politically while insisting that a period of decentralized judicial decision making will either resolve the issue or, if litigation falls short, provide useful policy experiments that will improve the design of future legislation.

As Congress stays on the sidelines, however, inefficient public policies and institutions create pressure for private actors and judges to develop new institutional arrangements by adapting existing rules and procedures on an ad hoc basis (Barnes 2008). Over time, the emergence of these subterranean practices and litigation strategies outside the Washington Beltway can erode the effectiveness of the politics of efficiency inside the Beltway in a variety of ways. They can provide partial exit strategies for individual actors that reduce the sense of urgency for comprehensive action, they can create their own support coalitions that oppose reform, and they can further balkanize the interests of stakeholder groups that otherwise would have been reform partners. In the case of asbestos, all these dynamics emerged. Politically, the net effect has been to help preserve the existing patchwork institutional response, to the collective detriment of thousands of business and millions of ordinary American workers and their families, who are silently suffering from what has been called "the worst industrial accident in US history" (Cauchon 1999, 4).

Chapter 6 brings the analysis full circle, returning to the broader issue of the prospects for reform in an age of polarized parties, slim majorities, and supermajority procedural hurdles in the Senate. It argues that, if nothing else, the asbestos case teaches us that federal policy emerges from interactions among the branches of government and that focusing on the actions of any single branch can be deceptive. With respect to institutional change, a narrow congressional focus in the case of asbestos would stress how multiple veto points in the Senate thwarted reform efforts, ostensibly reinforcing the conventional wisdom that the fragmented policymaking process in the United States protects the status quo and offers limited opportunities for significant reform. (Appendixes A, B, and C, respectively, give the details of the case method and "likely" cases, list a chronology of selected events, and offer questions for classroom discussion.)

Yet the asbestos case is a story of institutional change, not stability. As discussed throughout the book, the absence of major legislation has masked major judicial innovations that have transformed the scope and nature of asbestos injury compensation since the late 1960s—a point that resonates with a burgeoning literature on the judicialization of American politics (Schuck 1986; Melnick 1983, 1994; Rabkin 1989; Kagan 2001; Burke 2002; Farhang 2010) and the evolution of welfare states both here and abroad (see, e.g., Mahoney and Thelen 2010; Streeck and Thelen 2005; Hacker 2002, 2004; Thelen 2003; Schickler 2001; Clemens and Cook 1999; Weir 1992). In conclusion, it is argued that the dynamics of judicialization and the emergence of these subtle mechanisms of change are central to understanding the scope and nature of policymaking and institutional development in today's politics. Indeed, until we better grasp how legislative inertia coexists and even stimulates change in other forums, often through the adaptation and conversion of existing rules and policies by private actors and the courts, we are likely to underestimate the American political system's capacity for change and, in the process, miss important policy developments that unfold outside the spotlight of public or media attention and the din of high-profile partisan clashes on Capitol Hill (Hacker 2002, 2004).

NOTES

1. In the House, these were the 86th Congress (1959–61), 283 seats; 87th (1961–63), 262; 89th (1965–67), 295; 94th (1975–77), 291; 95th (1977–79), 292; 96th (1979–81), 277; 98th (1983–85), 269; and 102nd (1991–93), 267. During this period, the Democrats held nearly 261 seats—60 percent of the total—in the 88th Congress (1963–65), 258 seats; 100th (1987–89), 258; 101st (1989–91), 260; and 103rd (1993–95), 258. In the Senate, the Democrats controlled 60 or more seats in the 86th through 90th Congresses (1959–69), 64, 64, 67, 68, and 64 seats, respectively; and 94th and 95th (1975–79), 61. They held 58 seats twice, in the 91st (1969–71) and 96th (1979–81) Congresses.

2. A filibuster is a parliamentary maneuver in which senators prevent a floor vote by extending debate indefinitely. The requirements to end debate in the Senate and thus defeat a filibuster have a rich and complex history. In 1917 President Woodrow Wilson successfully urged the Democratic Senate to adopt a rule for ending a filibuster (known as "cloture"). From 1917 to 1949, cloture required two-thirds of those voting. In 1949 the rule was changed to two-thirds of the entire Senate, but was changed back to two-thirds of those voting in 1959. After a series of filibusters by Southern Democrats in the 1960s over civil rights legislation, Democrats changed the cloture rules so that three-fifths of the sworn senators, usually sixty, can end debate. More recently, following the 2010 midterm elections, Democrats considered a number of proposals that would have made filibusters somewhat more difficult. Ultimately, these reforms failed but the Senate agreed to modify some other delaying tactics, such as "secret holds," which allowed individual Senators to block legislation and nominations anonymously. For more on filibusters and cloture, see Beth, Heitshusen, and Palmer (2010).

3. As we will see in later chapters, members of the House or Senate may raise budgetary points of order against a bill or amendment if it violates spending or revenue levels contained in the most recent budget resolution or other rules governing the budgeting process. In the House, points of order can be waived by a simple majority; however, in the Senate, most require sixty votes to waive. If the point of order is not waived, the bill or amendment cannot be considered on the floor.

4. Filibusters have become so ingrained in the daily practice of the Senate that Common Cause, a public interest group, has challenged their constitutionality on the grounds that they undermine the principle of majority rule in the Senate (*Los Angeles Times* 2010).

5. The current ideological division is not unprecedented. Using Poole and Rosenthal's scores, parties in Congress were even more polarized in the second half of the nineteenth century and today's polarization follows a period of unusual party alignment on the liberal–conservative dimension. But the precipitous increase in the gap between the parties in Congress since the 1970s is unprecedented, and this rise has "left the House and the Senate with the most divergent and internally homogeneous party coalitions in living memory" (Jacobson 2007, 25).

6. Budget reconciliation stems from a provision in the 1974 Congressional Budget Act, which is designed to expedite the consideration of legislation concerning the budget and tax revenues. Specifically, a budget reconciliation bill is used to match federal policy with congressional fiscal guidelines. Under the procedures for reconciliation bills, debate is limited to 20 hours in each chamber of Congress and filibusters are not allowed. The process was intended to focus on proposals aimed at dealing with budget deficits. Under Senate rules devised by Senator Robert Byrd (D-WV), provisions in reconciliation bills whose fiscal effects are "merely incidental" can be struck out. (This vetting of provisions is known as giving the bill a "Byrd Bath.") Both political parties have used this process to pass major tax legislation, including President Bill Clinton's 1994 deficit reduction and tax plan and President George W. Bush's tax cuts. It has also been used to pass some social legislation, as when congressional Republicans used reconciliation to pass welfare reform in 1996.

CHAPTER 2

The Asbestos Crisis in the United States

To understand the most recent congressional attempt to address asbestos injury compensation issues and its broader implications, it is useful to gain a firmer grasp on the underlying asbestos crisis in the United States. This chapter provides the necessary background, though it needs to be noted here that a detailed exploration of this problem could fill an entire book by itself.[1] Accordingly, the chapter proceeds thematically by offering a thumbnail sketch of the rise of asbestos consumption and litigation in the United States, the growing critiques of asbestos litigation, the emergence of the politics of efficiency in connection with asbestos injury compensation issues, and the institutional response leading up to congressional efforts to pass major asbestos litigation reform following the 2004 elections. Some of this material is technical, because it takes the analysis into the nooks and crannies of complex litigation strategies and corporate reorganizations. Yet these details are essential because, as will be shown in later chapters, litigation and legislation are inextricably tied in the case of asbestos, and thus one cannot be fully understood without the other.

ASBESTOS CONSUMPTION IN THE UNITED STATES

Asbestos is a wonder material.[2] It is literally a fiber made of rock, which is waterproof, fireproof, and stronger than steel (Bowker 2003; Virta 2003). Asbestos is also abundant, cheap to mine, and amazingly versatile. As the United States industrialized throughout the twentieth century, entrepreneurs found new ways to use this "magic mineral" (Tweedale 2000), and its consumption skyrocketed (Virta 2003, 4). In 1900 Americans used about 20,000 metric tons of asbestos. By the 1930s, average annual consumption had increased more than eight times, to 170,550 metric tons, as manufacturers discovered, among other things, how to use asbestos-reinforced concrete to mass produce building materials and how to incorporate asbestos fibers into automobile parts, such as brakes and clutches. Consumption further accelerated during and after World War II. During the 1950s, Americans used an average of 672,900 metric tons of asbestos each year in more than 3,000 applications. The use of asbestos peaked in 1973, when the United States utilized 803,000 metric tons in everything from hair dryers to missile silos, home gardening products, and children's modeling clay (see fig. 2.1).

The problem is that asbestos can be lethal. Exposure to asbestos can cause mesothelioma, a deadly cancer of the lining of the chest or abdomen; asbestosis, a progressive and potentially fatal scarring of the lungs; and lung and larynx cancer (IOM 2006; Roggli, Oury, and Sporn 2004; NIOSH 2003, 2008). In addition, asbestos can produce pulmonary abnormalities, such as pleural plaques and thickening.[3] These abnormalities may—or may not—develop into serious illnesses. But even if they do not take a turn for the worse, their discovery can subject victims to years of stressful uncertainty about their health, because many of the worst asbestos-related diseases can take twenty to forty years to appear.

Calculating the final health toll in the United States from asbestos remains uncertain and may be impossible for a variety of reasons. Some of the dangers of asbestos are still disputed, especially in connection with some diseases, such as pharyngeal, stomach, colorectal, and esophageal cancers (IOM 2006); reliable historical data on asbestos-related deaths and illnesses are unavailable, in part because many workers suffering from asbestos-related diseases were probably misdiagnosed or not diagnosed at all; and many asbestos-related illnesses have long latency periods that complicate statistical projections.

We do know that the scope of the problem is staggering. Tens of millions of workers in high-risk industries and occupations—such as asbestos manufacturing, shipbuilding, construction, insulation workers, and automobile repair—were exposed during the peak years of consumption from 1940 and 1979 (Nicholson, Perkel, and Selikoff 1982). When these workers came home covered in toxic dust, they unwittingly endangered their families and greatly multiplied the number of people exposed. Meanwhile, in the mid-1980s, the US Environmental Protection Agency found asbestos in more than 733,000 public and commercial buildings and estimated that asbestos in schools affected 15 million children and 4.1 million school workers (EPA 1985; see also Ausness 1994; Lang 1985).

Figure 2.1. US Consumption of Asbestos in Metric Tons, 1900–2000 (in thousands)

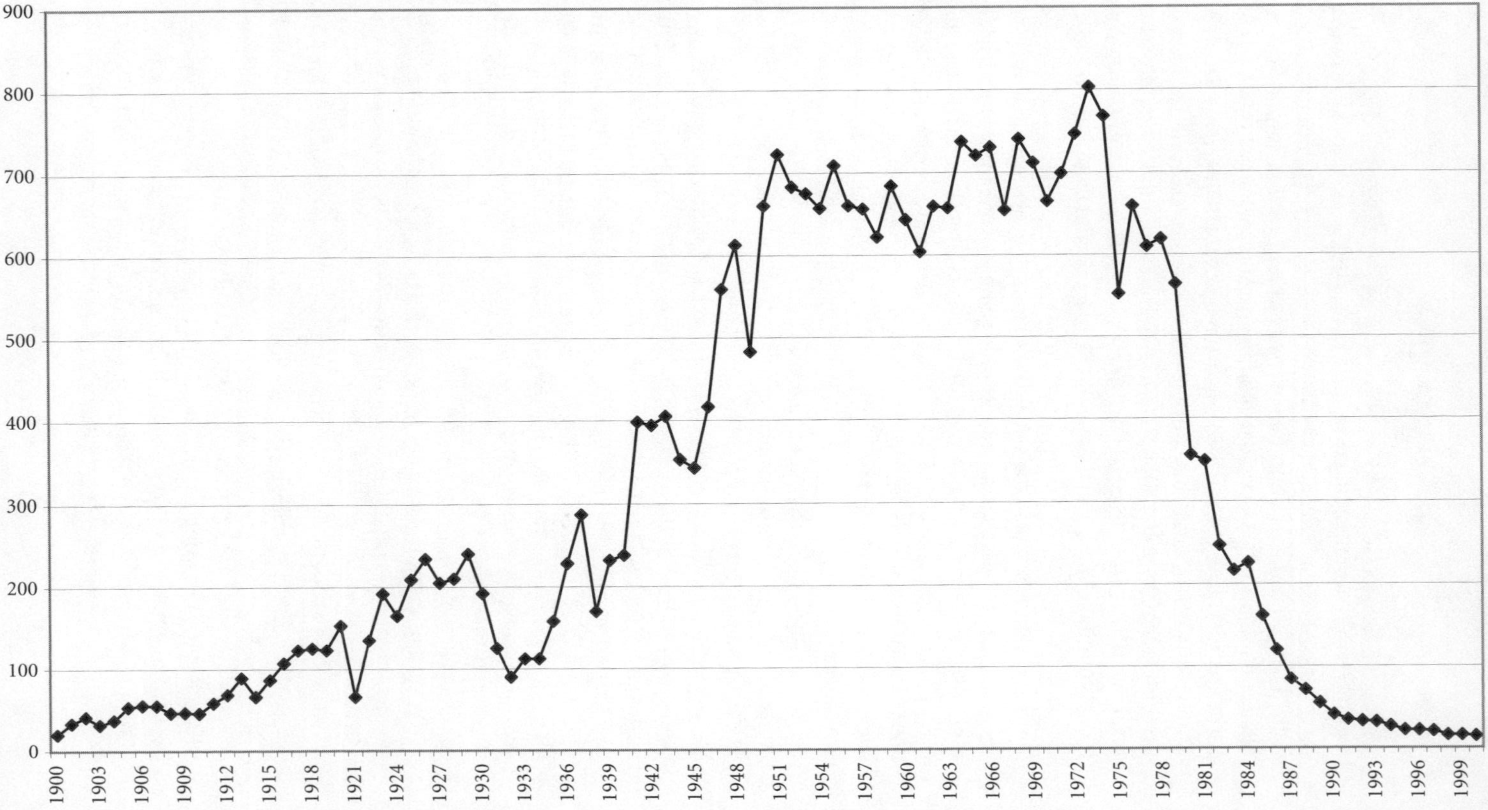

Given the long latency periods of many asbestos-related diseases, we are only now seeing the health effects of its pervasive use. Widely cited reports estimate that asbestos-related cancers have caused between 55,000 and 77,000 deaths in the past thirty years (cf. Walker et al. 1983 with Lilienfeld et al. 1988). Recently, the National Institute for Occupational Safety and Health (NIOSH) reported that asbestosis deaths had increased nearly twenty-fold from the late 1960s to the early 2000s and have surpassed black lung disease as the most frequent type of pneumoconioisis that causes death in the United States (NIOSH 2003, xxiii, and tables 1–1, 2–1, and 6–1 therein). Data on mesothelioma are scarcer, but the available information is equally sobering. NIOSH found that mesothelioma cost Americans aged fifteen years and above more than 32,000 years of potential life in 1999 alone (NIOSH 2003, table 7–3) and that mesothelioma-caused deaths are on the rise (NIOSH 2003, 2008).

It is worth noting that attempts to quantify the asbestos crisis have tended to *underestimate* the problem. Moreover, even if accurate, numbers cannot adequately convey the scale of human suffering. Asbestos has decimated entire communities, such as Libby, Montana, where vermiculite mining operations covered the town, including its Little League baseball diamond, with toxic amounts of asbestos dust (Bowker 2003). And the individual costs are incalculable. Alan Whitehouse, a physician in western Washington state, described asbestos-related diseases as "much worse than AIDS" (quoted by Bowker 2003, 109). Pat Cohen, clinic coordinator for Libby's Center for Asbestos-Related Diseases, describes the effects of asbestosis as follows: "Every time a patient with asbestosis takes a breath—which happens about sixteen to twenty times a minute—it rubs a sore spot. Your lungs just can't expand. You may be okay watching television, but if you get up to get yourself a cup of coffee in the kitchen, you suddenly run out of breath. Many asbestosis victims can't even get across the room. They sleep in a chair at night so they can breathe. It is a slow, strangulating process, and there is nothing anybody can do about it" (quoted by Bowker, 2003, 117).

Unfortunately, asbestos exposure is a continuing risk, not a historical concern. Although consumption has sharply declined since the 1970s, asbestos is still used legally in the United States, unlike in most other industrial democracies (Bowker 2003).[4] In 2000 Americans consumed about 14,600 tons of asbestos in hundreds of new products, including building materials, protective clothing, and replacement brake linings (Virta 2003, 6, table 2; see also fig. 2.1 above). Only time will tell if today's asbestos-containing products will become tomorrow's pathogens.

Moreover, banning the use of asbestos tomorrow would not eliminate its health risks. Tons of asbestos remain in older buildings and other structures that can be released during demolition or remodeling. The terrorist attacks of September 11, 2001, dramatically illustrated this possibility, when the collapse of the World Trade Center towers released a cloud of dust that exposed thousands to asbestos (Bowker 2003). Asbestos also occurs naturally. An EPA study found that biking, playing baseball, and other everyday recreational activities stirred up a particularly toxic form of asbestos dust in a park in El Dorado Hills, a town in northern California. Although some dismissed the EPA report as alarmist, a later peer-reviewed study found that the odds of mesothelioma increased significantly for those living near asbestos-containing rocks in California, suggesting that asbestos from natural sources should not be ignored as a public health risk (Pan et al. 2005).

Not surprisingly, the costs related to asbestos exposure are mounting. The RAND Institute for Civil Justice finds that industry had spent more than $70 billion on asbestos claims as of 2002, forcing more than seventy companies into bankruptcy (Carroll et al. 2002, xxvi; 2005). These costs hurt not only management but also workers. A team of economists led by the Nobel laureate Joseph Stiglitz estimated that asbestos-related bankruptcies could cost as many as 423,000 jobs, while the average value of these firms' pensions dropped 25 percent (Stiglitz, Orzag, and Orzag 2002). A 2001 study estimated that the final price tag could reach $265 billion (Bhagavatula, Moody, and Russ 2001) or more than $328 billion adjusted for inflation, which is larger than the entire 2009 gross national income of Switzerland, the world's fifteenth-largest economy by that measure. Using these figures, we may be less than one-third of the way through the problem of compensating the victims of asbestos exposure.

TURNING TO THE COURTS FOR COMPENSATION, AND THE STORY OF CLARENCE BOREL

Asbestos injury compensation issues began to gain national prominence in the early 1960s, when American asbestos workers and their families who had been exposed during World War II began falling ill in increasing numbers. At that time, workers, if they sought compensation at all, turned to state workers' compensation programs. Under these no-fault employer-responsibility programs, workers do not need to prove that their employer was negligent, and employers cannot sidestep liability by arguing that workers assumed the risk or contributed to their injuries. Instead, employers are absolutely liable for workers' medical costs and also for approximately two-thirds of their weekly wages (subject to certain limits and offsets). Claims are adjudicated by administrative tribunals, whose decisions could be appealed to state appellate courts.

By the 1960s, workers' compensation programs had become fiercely adversarial and legalistic (Nonet 1969; Brodeur 1986; Schroeder 1986; Kagan 2001). Although fault is not an issue, these programs afford ample grounds for contestation. Employers and their insurers can challenge whether injuries are work related; the extent of workers' disabilities; and whether claims meet a range of procedural requirements. In the case of asbestos, they fought workers' claims on all these grounds. Employers and insurers argued that smoking, not asbestos, caused workers' lung problems. They alleged that workers suffering from asbestosis—a slowly debilitating disease—were not "totally disabled," as required under many state laws. And they insisted that states' statutes of limitation barred many asbestos workers' claims, because these provisions (at the time) required claims to be filed within one to three years of an injury but many of the worst asbestos-related diseases took decades to appear.

As American asbestos workers grew frustrated with workers' compensation systems designed for traumatic injuries, such as broken arms and legs, and not for occupational diseases with long latency periods, such as asbestosis and mesothelioma, they could have pursued a range of options in the late 1960s. Following the example of coal miners, they could have mobilized collectively and lobbied Congress (or state legislatures) for a new compensation program along the lines of the Black Lung Disability Trust Fund, a government-run program for miners suffering from coal dust–related illnesses, which provides benefits according to detailed payment schedules and more lenient eligibility standards than state workers' compensation programs (Nelson 1985; Smith 1987; Derickson 1998). Instead, asbestos workers individually turned to the tort system, seeking compensation from third-party manufacturers that supplied asbestos-containing products to the workplace.

The story of Clarence Borel, whose lawsuit in the late 1960s marked a major turning point in modern asbestos litigation, illustrates how and why asbestos workers resorted to the legal system.[5] For more than thirty years, Borel had insulated steam pipes, boilers, and other high-temperature equipment in shipyards and oil refineries using asbestos-laden products in the "Golden Triangle" region, a heavily industrial area along the Sabine River that divides Texas and Louisiana.

For most of his life, Borel had enjoyed steady work and reasonably good health. By the mid-1960s, however, constant exposure to asbestos began to take its toll. In 1964, his doctors warned him that his lungs were cloudy and that he should avoid further exposure as much as possible (Gifford 2010, 47). Borel, the father of six children, continued to work as a pipe insulator, and his condition worsened. In January 1968 he developed pain in his chest and difficulty in breathing while working in a refinery for Fuller-Austin Insulation Company. Initially, he was diagnosed with pneumonia and sent to recuperate in a hospital in Port Arthur. During the next month, his condition deteriorated and doctors sent him to Houston for exploratory surgery. The surgery revealed the worst-case scenario; he was not only suffering from pneumonia but also had an advanced case of asbestosis. Later he would be diagnosed with mesothelioma. At the age of fifty-seven, Clarence Borel was dying.

Like many asbestos workers at the time, Borel did not initially file a lawsuit seeking compensation for his illnesses. Instead, in the spring of 1968, he filed a workers' compensation claim, which he eventually settled for $8,000 plus $5,081.10 in medical expenses—for a grand total of $13,081.10 for injuries that amounted to a death sentence. In August, he decided to visit an attorney, Ward Stephenson, to see if he could claim further compensation in the courts to help cover his ongoing medical expenses and provide for his family.

When Borel arrived in Stephenson's office, he was visibly ill—pale, gaunt, and short of breath. He admitted that he knew asbestos dust was unhealthy and that he refused to wear a respirator at work because they were uncomfortable and easily clogged (Gifford 2010, 45). Nevertheless, he insisted that he never knew that asbestos dust could be fatal because he assumed that it would dissolve upon entering his lungs. He also maintained that he was never adequately warned of the dangers of asbestos. Instead, beginning in 1964, long after he began working, asbestos products provided only generic warnings that "inhalation of asbestos in excessive quantities over longer periods of time may be harmful" (Gifford 2010, 47).

Borel's choice of Stephenson was fortunate. Stephenson was an experienced and innovative trial lawyer, who took cases on a contingency fee basis, meaning that Stephenson fronted the cost of litigation in exchange for a share—usually 30 to 40 percent—of any eventual verdict or settlement. In addition, Stephenson was one of a handful of attorneys in the late 1960s with experience in asbestos litigation, because he had recently settled a case for $75,000 on behalf of another pipe insulator, Claude L. Tomplait.

Fresh from his success in the Tomplait litigation, Stephenson wasted no time in preparing Borel's case. Before Borel left his office, Stephenson told his new client to review his tax records and carefully reconstruct his employment history. Stephenson was in luck; unlike Tomplait, whose poor records had proved a hindrance in his case, Borel was able to create a detailed list of his jobs and when he used asbestos-containing products, although pinpointing which products proved fatal was simply not possible given the cumulative nature of his injuries.

The confluence of two events in the 1960s strengthened Stephenson's hand. One was medical. During 1962 and 1963, three doctors began studying mortality rates among asbestos-insulation workers: Irving Selikoff of Mount Sinai School of Medicine; Jacob Churg, chief pathologist at Barnert Memorial Hospital; and E. Cuyler Hammond, vice president for epidemiology and statistics of the American Cancer Society (Selikoff et al. 1965). In October 1964, they presented their findings at an international conference on the biological effects of asbestos sponsored by the New York Academy of Sciences. These studies provided a strong scientific basis for Stephenson's claim that asbestos had caused Borel's illnesses.

The other was legal. In the spring of 1965, the American Law Institute published the second edition of its *Restatement of the Law of Torts*, which culminated years of effort to clarify tort law by a leading group of law professors, judges, and lawyers. Section 402A of the *Restatement* set forth a new theory of products liability law, called "strict product liability." It stated: "One who sells any product in a defective condition unreasonably dangerous to the user or consumer or to his property is subject to liability for physical harm thereby caused to the ultimate user or consumer," even if the seller "has exercised all possible care in the preparation and sale of his product." The *Restatement* went on to explain that unavoidably unsafe products would not be considered unreasonably dangerous as long as they were "properly prepared, and accompanied by proper directions and warning."[6] Before Borel's case, Texas had adopted Section 402A, which seemed a promising theory for suing asbestos manufacturers and mining companies on the grounds that they provided inadequate warnings in connection with their products containing asbestos.

Armed with Borel's detailed work records, Dr. Selikoff and his associates' medical findings, and Section 402A, Stephenson formally commenced Borel's lawsuit by filing a complaint in federal court for the Eastern District of Texas against eleven asbestos manufacturers from across the United States. The complaint sought $1 million in damages under Section 402A's theory of strict product liability for failing to warn.[7]

Clarence Borel never saw his day in court. He died on June 3, 1970. However, under Texas law, his wife, Thelma, was able to take his place and the lawsuit proceeded. After a hotly contested trial, the Borels prevailed, winning damages of $79,436.24. It was the first time that a court held asbestos manufacturers strictly liable for failing to provide sufficient warnings about their products' health risks.

In the American legal system, winning at trial is only the first step in the litigation process. The losers can appeal and that is exactly what the defendants did in the Borel case. Leaving no stone unturned, the manufacturers hired W. Page Keeton to argue their case before the Fifth Circuit of the US Courts of Appeal. Keeton was the dean of the University of Texas Law School, a leading expert on torts, and one of the architects of Section 402A. Keeton argued that the district court had erred as a matter of law, maintaining that strict liability should not be imposed simply because harm was reasonably foreseeable from a product's ordinary use. After all, harm is foreseeable from the use of almost any product, including cars, knives, stoves, and penicillin—and the list goes on. Using Keeton's academic writings, Stephenson countered that it would be absurd to allow manufacturers to avoid liability by turning a blind eye to their products' dangers and concealing public health risks (Brodeur 1986, 66–68).

On September 10, 1973, in an opinion by the marvelously named Judge John Minor Wisdom, the Fifth Circuit rejected the manufacturers' appeal and affirmed the lower court.[8] In siding with Borel, Judge Wisdom leaned heavily on the manufacturers' failure to provide adequate warnings of the dangers of asbestos, stating as follows: "In reaching our decision in the case at bar, we recognize that the question of the applicability of Section 402A of the Restatement to cases involving 'occupational diseases' is one of first impression. But though the application is novel, the underlying principle is ancient. Under the law of torts, a person has long been liable for the foreseeable harm caused by his own negligence. . . . It implies a duty to warn of foreseeable dangers. . . . This duty to warn extends to all users and consumers, including the common worker in the shop or in the field. . . . Here, there was a duty to speak, but the defendants remained silent" (*Borel v. Fibreboard Products Corporation*, at 1103). Although couched in terms of well-settled principles, the court's broad interpretation of Section 402A created a new policy that significantly increased the potential liability of manufacturers of inherently dangerous products, even if the users of these products contributed to their injuries, on the theory that manufacturers are in a better position to detect risks, avoid future harm, and broadly distribute the costs of injuries (Gifford 2010, 52).

Given the potential stakes of this new policy, it is not surprising that the defendants continued to fight. They asked for a rehearing but the Fifth Circuit refused (*Borel*, at 1109). They then appealed to the US Supreme Court, but the Court denied their petition (419 US 869 1974). After these options were exhausted, the Borel litigation finally came to a close. Other federal appellate courts followed suit, and they held that asbestos manufacturing and mining companies could be held strictly liable under Section 402A (see, e.g., *Karjala v. Johns-Manville Products Corporation*; *Moran v. Johns-Manville Sales Corporation*). The legal foundation for modern asbestos litigation thus had been established, which would make it easier for other asbestos workers (and their attorneys) to use litigation to address asbestos injury compensation issues.

THE RISE OF ASBESTOS LITIGATION

The *Borel* legal victory, though important, did not automatically translate into compensation for claimants. Plaintiffs won only about half the cases that went to trial immediately following *Borel* (Brodeur 1986). The reason was that *Borel*'s "strict liability" standard was qualified and subject to various defenses. So, under *Borel*, companies were only obligated to warn about "reasonably foreseeable" dangers (*Borel*, at 1088) in connection with reasonably foreseeable applications (1090). The warnings needed only be "adequate" (1089) and "reasonably calculated to reach" the public (1091). Even if a seller acted unreasonably, the failure to warn must proximately cause the plaintiffs' injuries (1090). *Borel* also recognized the so-called state-of-the-art defense, which holds that sellers can only be liable for reasonably knowable risks, or the state of the art of existing medical and scientific knowledge (1089).[9]

Immediately following *Borel*, defendants typically asserted the state-of-the-art defense and claimed that they were unaware of the health risks associated with asbestos before the publication of studies by Dr. Selikoff and his colleagues in the mid-1960s. As such, early asbestos litigation often hinged on what companies knew and when they knew it. A critical turning point in this battle over the facts was the discovery of the "Sumner Simpson Papers" during litigation against Raybestos-Manhattan, which was one of the largest asbestos manufacturers in the United States (Castleman 2005). The story is that Karl Asch, who represented asbestos workers at Raybestos-Manhattan's Passaic plant, obtained a routine subpoena in February 1977 ordering William Simpson, president of Raybestos and son of its founder,

Sumner Simpson, to testify at a deposition and bring any documents pertaining to the plant's working conditions. During the deposition, Asch asked whether the company had hired any independent consultants to study the health effects of asbestos and, if so, whether there were any documents related to these studies. Defense attorneys directed him to a seemingly innocuous box of Sumner Simpson's personal papers, which his son had dutifully saved. The box contained a treasure trove of correspondence between Sumner Simpson and his counterparts at other leading asbestos manufacturer companies, which showed that these companies not only knew about the risks of asbestos for decades but also had commissioned studies on its dangers and concealed the results. Asch knew that he had "hit pay dirt" (quoted by Brodeur 1986, 111).

"Pay dirt" is right. The uncovering of the Sumner Simpson papers and similar evidence exposed decades of willful corporate misconduct in concealing public health risks, destroyed the state-of-the-art defense, and unleashed a torrent of successful (and highly lucrative) litigation. As of 2002, an estimated 730,000 individual claims for asbestos-related injuries had been filed in the United States, and the number of annual claims is still climbing (Carroll et al. 2002, xxiv; 2005). These suits have targeted more than 8,400 firms, including at least one company in seventy-five of the eighty-three categories of economic activity in the Standard Industrial Classification, which seeks to categorize all types of business activity within the economy (Carroll et al. 2002, xxv; 2005). In 2002, *Barron's* named forty publicly traded companies with significant, and growing, asbestos-liability exposure (Abelson 2002). The list reads like a corporate *Who's Who*, including Dow Chemical, DaimlerChrysler, Ford, IBM, Kaiser Aluminum, Pfizer, Sears, Viacom, and even Disney.

It is important to stress that many of these companies had little or nothing to do with concealing the dangers of asbestos; they merely used asbestos-containing products in their businesses or had acquired firms that had once produced asbestos or used products. Pacor, Incorporated, offers a case in point. In the 1980s Pacor was a medium-sized insulation company with annual sales of about $20 million. Pacor did not mine asbestos or manufacture asbestos products. It merely purchased insulation materials from the leading asbestos manufacturers and relied on them to supply high-quality, safe products. James E. Sullivan, Pacor's chairman, explained to Congress as follows: "We purchased insulation products from reputable manufacturers and used them in our business without any conception of their danger. We relied on manufacturers to test their products and make sure they were safe, as much as we rely on automobile manufacturers to test their vehicles and the ladder manufacturers to test their ladders. Purchasers like insulation contractors simply do not have the money or expertise to fully evaluate the composition and safety features of every product they purchase" (House Committee on Labor Standards 1983, 45).

Nevertheless, under the rules of the tort system, Pacor faced thousands of asbestos-related claims. As a consequence of litigation, Pacor lost its insurance and credit rating. In 1983, Sullivan urged Congress to act; he argued that "there has to be some sort of global solution to the asbestos problem pretty soon, or most of us will not make it" (House Committee on Labor Standards 1983, 45). Three years later, as Sullivan predicted, asbestos litigation overwhelmed Pacor, and it filed for bankruptcy. On top of the failure of his company, Sullivan was diagnosed with mesothelioma and joined the ranks of thousands of asbestos victims, like Claude Tomplait and Clarence Borel, who had unwittingly endangered their lives by using asbestos products at work.

A cross-national comparison with the Netherlands helps place the American experience in perspective. According to comparative legal scholars, the incidence of asbestos-related diseases was five to ten times higher in Dutch workers in the 1970s and 1980s, and, unlike American law, which channels most employee claims against their employers into workers' compensation programs, Dutch law allows workers to bring tort suits directly against their employers (Vinke and Wilthagen 1992). Yet only *ten* tort suits had reportedly been filed in the Netherlands as of 1991. By contrast, one of every three civil cases filed in the Eastern District of Texas in 1990 was an asbestos case (Judicial Conference Ad Hoc Committee 1991, 8). The reason for this discrepancy, Vinke and Wilthagen argue, is that Dutch workers received adequate compensation from their relatively generous social benefit programs, rendering tort actions largely unnecessary. Whatever the reason, there is little doubt that the American institutional response to the asbestos crisis has been remarkably litigious and stands in stark contrast to other countries. The question is whether asbestos litigation has represented an effective and efficient means of responding to the underlying policy problem.

THE GROWING CRITIQUES
OF ASBESTOS LITIGATION

In the late 1960s and early 1970s asbestos litigation undoubtedly served important, even heroic, policy functions (Brodeur 1986; Bowker 2003;

Barnes 2009a; see, generally, Mather 1998; Bogus 2001; Frymer 2003). For ordinary workers like Clarence Borel and Claude Tomplait, the courts provided a forum for raising concerns when other branches and levels of government were not responsive. Once established, asbestos litigation provided a means for bypassing the limited state workers' compensation programs, increasing awareness of the dangers of asbestos, and uncovering decades of corporate wrongdoing.

Over time, however, as the policy cycle shifted from agenda setting, mobilization, and information gathering on the issue of fault to the creation and implementation of a comprehensive compensation program for asbestos victims, many experts began to raise serious doubts about the costs and fairness of asbestos litigation. A 1983 RAND study showed that asbestos plaintiffs received only 37 cents of every dollar spent to resolve asbestos claims, which is significantly less than ordinary tort claims (Kakalik et al. 1983). Recent follow-up studies have shown that these patterns have persisted because administrative costs still consume more than half of all compensation paid (Hensler et al. 2001; Carroll et al. 2002, 2005). By contrast, the administrative costs of the Black Lung Disability Trust Fund, which are often criticized as excessive, accounted for only 4.5 percent to 5.8 percent of the program's annual obligations from 1992 to 2006 (Office of Workers' Compensation 2001; 2007, table B-4).

These costs might be tolerable if asbestos litigation delivered consistent compensation, but it has been erratic. In Texas, five juries in a multiplaintiff trial heard exactly the same evidence and ruled differently on specific liability and causation issues (Bell and O'Connell 1997, 22). Jury damage awards also have varied from case to case and jurisdiction to jurisdiction, providing similarly situated plaintiffs with different amounts of compensation and giving those with harder-to-prove claims nothing at all (Sugarman 1989, 46). Meanwhile, some claimants who were herded into massive class action settlements have been limited to lower recoveries than those who sued individually or had happened to be swept into earlier class action settlements (Coffee 1995, 1384–96), while payments to claimants of Chapter 11 trusts have varied according to the solvency of the underlying trust as opposed to the merit of the claims (Barnes 2007b; Austern 2001).

Asbestos litigation is also slow because cases can languish in the courts for years while claimants grow increasingly ill and some, like Clarence Borel, die before they see a penny of compensation (Hensler et al. 1985, 84–65; see also Carroll et al. 2002, 2005). Even worse, asbestos litigation now reportedly features dubious claiming practices that, in some instances, have placed the interests of lawyers above their clients and the needs of the "worried well"—those who have been exposed to asbestos but have not (yet) fallen ill—before the dying (see Koniak 1995; Coffee 1995; Carrington 2007; Hanlon 2006; *Mealey's Litigation Report: Asbestos Bankruptcy* 2005; Carroll et al. 2002, 2005; Schuck 1992; Huber 1991).

THE POLITICS OF EFFICIENCY AND ASBESTOS LITIGATION

As critiques of asbestos litigation multiplied, the politics of efficiency emerged at the center of the battle over asbestos injury compensation issues, as reformers framed the need for legislation in terms of the short-comings of litigation. In 1982, for instance, the leading proponent for asbestos reform in Congress, Representative George Miller (D-CA), maintained that a federal asbestos-injury compensation fund was necessary because the existing system "failed to meet the needs of occupational disease victims" (Occupational Health Hazards Compensation Act of 1982 Hearings 1982, 93). The following year, Representative Miller convened a special hearing on the effect of bankruptcy cases and private settlements, arguing that the "testimony we will hear this morning will further establish the need to replace years of failure with a compensation system that can meet the needs of the disabled asbestos workers" (House Subcommittee on Labor Standards 1983, 2).

These arguments were echoed outside Congress. The leading study of asbestos litigation in the mid-1980s argued that "whether one believes that alternatives to the tort system, such as those proposed in recent legislation introduced by Congressmen George Miller and others, are necessary, should rest in part on an assessment of how well the tort system has processed asbestos claims" (Hensler et al. 1985, 4–5). The courts picked up these arguments as well. In the early 1990s a special committee of the Judicial Conference sharply criticized litigation's inefficiency and inconsistency as a means of compensation and recommended that Congress replace it with a "national asbestos-dispute resolution scheme" (Judicial Conference Ad Hoc Committee 1991, 3, 27–35). In *Amchem Products v. Windsor*, *Ortiz v. Fibreboard*, and *Norfolk & Western Railway Co. v. Ayers*, the Supreme Court reinforced these recommendations, directly urging Congress to act on the grounds that "the elephantine mass of asbestos cases . . . defies customary judicial administration and calls for national legislation" (*Ortiz*, at 821).

THE INSTITUTIONAL RESPONSE TO DATE

As the shortcomings of asbestos litigation as a means of compensation grew, pressure mounted for change. In the fragmented US system of policy-making, this pressure has been felt in both legislatures and courts, which has resulted in multiple layers of legislative and judicial reform efforts. Each is reviewed here.

Legislative Response

Given the emergence of the politics of efficiency in asbestos compensation issues, it is not surprising that legislative activity has waxed and waned depending on the perceived effectiveness of asbestos litigation. This dynamic was particularly salient in the mid-1980s, when many felt that asbestos litigation had become a "mature" mass tort and provided adequate means of asbestos-related claims. A prominent Washington lawyer and lobbyist explained, "You stop getting bills around 1986 . . . [because] everyone thought that this was really a solved problem. The coverage issues were largely resolved; the people were getting into agreements that processed them more or less administratively."[10] Consistent with this assessment, major reform proposals aimed at replacing asbestos litigation with administrative alternatives dropped off during this period (see fig. 2.2). But they reappeared on Congress's agenda in the 1990s, after it became clear that the courts alone could not resolve the asbestos crisis for a variety of reasons—including the continuing drumbeat of large verdicts in some jurisdictions; the rejection of mandatory class action lawsuits as a tool for creating large settlements by the Supreme Court; the collapse of major private settlements, such as the Owens-Corning settlement; and the growing costs associated with using bankruptcy as a means to manage asbestos litigation liability (discussed below).

During the spurts of legislative activity, federal and state reformers advanced three main types of reform proposals (see, generally, Burke 2002, 27–44, and table 1.1): *discouragement reforms*, such as caps on damage awards, that aim to deter asbestos lawsuits by making them harder to pursue or potentially less remunerative; *management reforms*, such as mandatory arbitration and uniform codes that clarify rules, which are designed to make disputing more efficient and less adversarial; and *replacement reforms*, such as no-fault compensation trust funds, which offer an administrative alternative to litigation.

Figure 2.2. Number of Replacement Reforms, 93rd to 109th Congresses, 1974–2008

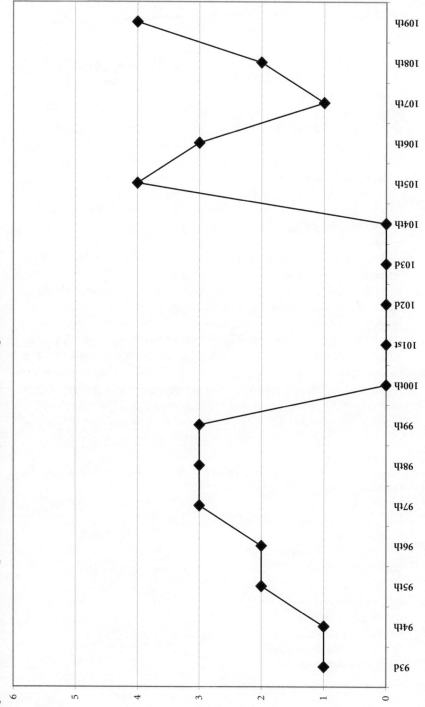

Source: Compiled by the author from Thomas Bill summaries.

At the federal level, Congress has done more talking than legislating. A search of the Congressional Information Service's congressional hearing abstracts and the Library of Congress's Thomas Bill summaries from 1973 to today reveals more than thirty-five hearings and fifty significant bills on asbestos-compensation issues. Yet Congress has enacted only one bill into law: the Bankruptcy Amendments of 1994, which, among other things, retroactively approved the bankruptcy court's power to issue "channeling injunctions," court orders that direct future litigation from a reorganized company to private trust funds. In other words, far from reforming the system, the only major federal law passed to date codified existing practices and seemingly strengthened the courts' grip on asbestos compensation issues.

With Congress staying on the sidelines, the states have taken some action by enacting or considering a whole host of discouragement reforms, which have imposed new hurdles on plaintiffs and have limited the damages they can win (see table 2.1). These state measures, however, only provide a piecemeal response to a national problem and, according to leading practitioners, can often be circumvented through "forum shopping," as plaintiffs facing legal obstacles in one jurisdiction file a suit in another, more lenient jurisdiction. Equally important, discouragement reforms, by definition, do not provide an alternative to litigation or even seek to streamline the litigation process. They aim to deter the amount of litigation by impeding the filing of suits and making them potentially less

Table 2.1.   Examples of Enacted or Proposed State Asbestos Litigation Reforms, as of the 109th Congress

Reform	States
Punitive damage caps	AK, ID, SC, NM, MS, OH
Noneconomic damage caps	MS, OH
Caps on appeal bonds	AK, CO, ID, MO, NC, TN, TX, GA, IA, MN, NE
Limits on pre- and postjudgment interest	GA, IA, ME, TX, OK, WA
Settlement/fee-shifting bills	CO, TX
Limits on joint and several liability	ID, MS, MN, TX, OK
Limits on product liability	CO, MS, TX
Curbs on forum shopping	AK, GA, WV, TX, MS

Source: Barnes 2007b.

lucrative while leaving many structural features that drive tort litigation firmly in place. The bottom line is that the legislative response has been limited, working on the margins of a vast amount of asbestos litigation that has a seemingly endless capacity for reinventing and rejuvenating itself (White 2002, 2004, 2005).

Court-Based Tort Reforms

We tend to assume that either Congress or the state legislatures must enact tort reform. However, judges can implement "court-based tort reform"— that is, the adaptation of existing rules and procedures that significantly changes the basic structure of who decides, who pays, how much, and to whom (Barnes 2007b; see generally Ursin 1981). Indeed, in the case of asbestos, judges and lawyers have been remarkably resourceful in implementing their own brand of ad hoc discouragement, management, and replacement reforms, which aim to regulate the flow of cases, make the adjudication process less adversarial and more efficient, and offer administrative alternatives to tort litigation (see table 2.2 for a side-by-side comparison). These judicial innovations, though somewhat arcane, are an essential feature of the institutional landscape of asbestos injury compensation in the United States and the politics of asbestos litigation reform. As such, it is worth delving into a few examples to make matters more concrete.[11]

Court-Based Discouragement Reform

Judges can implement court-based discouragement reform and chill litigation by construing tort law narrowly. Some have argued that popular disapproval of tort law may have caused judges to implement a "quiet revolution" in products liability law that has made it harder for plaintiffs to bring and win these claims (Eisenberg and Henderson 1992; Henderson and Eisenberg 1990; but see Schwartz 1992). In asbestos, courts may have begun limiting the reach of some tort theories used in asbestos litigation, such as dismissing claims by family members of asbestos workers (compare *Holdampf v. A.C. & S., Inc. [In the Matter of New York City Asbestos Litigation]* and *CSX Transportation, Inc. v. Williams* with *Olivio v. Owens-Illinois, Inc.*). In addition, courts have made it more difficult to prove some types of claims by raising the requirements for expert testimony (*Daubert v. Merrell Dow Pharmaceuticals, Inc.*; *Mealey's Litigation Report: Asbestos Bankruptcy* 2005).

Table 2.2. Overview of Legislative versus Court-Based Tort Reform

Type of Reform	Definition	Examples of Legislative Tort Reform	Examples of Court-Based Tort Reform
Discouragement	Actions that seek to deter the filing of lawsuits by making them harder to bring or potentially less remunerative	Damage caps	Narrow interpretation of tort doctrine, inactive dockets
Management	Actions that seek to streamline the adjudication process by clarifying the law and making procedures more efficient and less adversarial	Legislative overrides (aimed at clarifying conflicting interpretations of statutes)	Pretrial discovery orders, collateral estoppel, multidistrict litigation
Replacement	Actions that create administrative alternatives to litigation	No-fault trust funds	Chapter 11 compensation trusts

Source: Barnes 2007b.

More subtly, judges have implemented court-based discouragement reform through their inherent powers to manage dockets. Specifically, they have issued standing orders that have created inactive dockets, which are also known as pleural registries, unimpaired-asbestos dockets, and deferred dockets (see, generally, Behrens and Lopez 2005; Schuck 1992; Hensler et al. 1985; and see, e.g., *In re USG Corp.*; *Sophia v. Owens-Corning Fiberglass*; and *In re Report of the Advisory Group*). Similar to all discouragement reforms, these orders do not change the underlying litigation process for active claims once the process begins. Instead they raise the bar for pursuing asbestos-related claims by requiring them to meet more stringent medical standards than ordinary tort suits. The result is a two-tiered system in which qualified claims go forward under existing rules and procedures but others must wait until the claimant's health meets the relevant medical criteria, which for some lawsuits indefinitely delay "discovery"—the process through which lawyers gather evidence for trial—which can hinder the development of claims and the reaching of settlements.

Court-Based Management Reform

Judges have also implemented a variety of court-based management reforms designed to streamline the litigation process. A leading innovator was Judge Robert M. Parker, who was appointed in 1979 to the Federal District Court of the Eastern District of Texas, the home of the Golden Triangle, where Clarence Borel and Claude Tomplait worked as insulators (McGovern 1989; Barnes 2007b). In 1982 Parker issued a standing pretrial order for his courtroom that substantially limited the discretion of lawyers during discovery. Among other things, the order barred duplicative depositions; limited interrogatories to a single set of master questions that could be supplemented by court order only under "extraordinary circumstances"; preemptively ruled on a range of pretrial motions, including motions for summary judgment, regardless of whether the lawyers for individual clients filed such motions; and required lawyers to coordinate their efforts (*Hardy v. Johns-Manville Sales Corporation*).

Not limiting himself to the discovery process, Judge Parker consolidated individual trials to speed dispute resolution and enhance consistency. For example, he empanelled five juries to hear evidence on common issues in five cases at once, but while this may have saved courtroom time, it failed to standardize the outcomes because the juries divided on liability issues despite having heard the same evidence. Undaunted, the judge designated lead cases and aggressively applied the doctrines of collateral estoppel and judicial notice, rules that allowed him to designate certain issues as settled and thus not needing to be proved in subsequent cases. When these techniques were reversed on appeal (*Hardy*, at 334), he grouped thirty defendants for trial and had one jury decide common liability issues. Similar techniques were also used elsewhere (Hensler et al. 1985, 104–7).

Court-based management reform has not been confined to single court-rooms. As early as 1977, lawyers urged the Judicial Panel on Multidistrict Litigation (JPML) to centralize all federal asbestos litigation for pretrial purposes under a statutory provision, 28 U.S.C. §1407, which empowers the JPML to consolidate civil actions brought in different jurisdictions for pretrial proceedings if the actions involve at least one common question of fact and the transfer will be convenient and "promote the just and efficient conduct of such actions" (see, generally, Hensler 2001). The JPML initially refused to consolidate asbestos litigation on the grounds that pending actions presented too many unique factual issues and that pretrial consolidation would serve little purpose because many cases were close to trial (*In re Asbestos and Asbestos Material Products Liability Litigation*). The parties persisted, and, finally, after the Judicial Conference strongly endorsed consolidation in its 1991 report, the JPML ordered almost 27,000 federal cases to be transferred to the Eastern District of Pennsylvania for pretrial purposes.

Court-Based Replacement Reform

Judges have gone even further and implemented court-based replacement reforms, which have created quasi-administrative entities that compensate asbestos victims according to detailed medical criteria and preexisting payment schedules and thus provide an alternative to torts. The tools of court-based replacement reform include Chapter 11 bankruptcy reorganizations, group settlements, and, in some circumstances, class action lawsuits, cases in which individual claims that share similar legal and factual issues are consolidated into a single lawsuit.[12]

In the asbestos case, the paradigmatic example of court-based replacement reform was the Johns-Manville Corporation's bankruptcy. Johns-Manville was the leading asbestos mining-and-manufacturing company in the United States and a primary target of asbestos litigation. In 1982 Johns-Manville filed for reorganization under Chapter 11 of the bankruptcy code, even though it was a Fortune 500 company and its day-to-day operations were profitable. Johns-Manville defended its move on the grounds that mounting asbestos liability threatened its future solvency. Under these conditions, filing for bankruptcy promised several advantages commonly associated with any Chapter 11: It suspended pending litigation; it transferred all litigation to a single bankruptcy court, where there is no right to jury trial and the debtor's attorneys' fees are reviewed by the court; and it offered the company a chance to reorganize its business, preserve assets for the benefit of all of its creditors, and prioritize payments.

Johns-Manville's Chapter 11 process, however, did more than rationalize the payment of claims and reorganize the company. It created an entirely new administrative entity with its own source of funding and rulemaking authority, which was authorized not only to handle claims pending at the time of the company's bankruptcy but also to resolve future claims. Specifically, in 1986, after four long years of negotiation and litigation, the bankruptcy court confirmed Johns-Manville's first plan of reorganization, which featured two main components: the creation of the Asbestos Health Trust (hereafter, the Trust) and a channeling injunction, which directs all future asbestos litigation against Johns-Manville to the Trust and, thus, away from the newly reorganized company, called the Manville Corporation. The Trust was funded by Johns-Manville with cash, proceeds from various settlements with its liability-insurance companies, and stock in the new Manville Corporation.

The initial version of the Trust can be understood as a weak form of court-based replacement reform because it offered an alternative dispute resolution mechanism without actively directing claims away from the tort system. The Trust required claimants to first attempt to settle claims. If settlement failed, claimants could choose to arbitrate, mediate, or litigate their claims. The Trust promised claimants 100 percent of their settlement values and, in the case of tort litigation, 100 percent of their compensatory damages (out-of-pocket costs) but no punitive damages (penalties for misconduct). By 1990 the Trust became insolvent, in part because it underestimated the number of claims and in part because too many claimants opted for tort litigation, which produced higher-than-expected damage awards (Peterson 1990).

The Trust's financial collapse sent the parties back to the drawing board. After a hotly contested appeals process and a foray into Congress that resulted in the Bankruptcy Reform Amendments of 1994, which codified the use of channeling injunctions in asbestos-related bankruptcies, the new Trust began making distributions in 1996. Under the Trust's restructuring, several basic features of the original plan endured: The Trust continued to be funded with a large equity stake in the Manville Corporation, and the channeling injunction still directed all claims to the Trust and away from the reorganized company.

Other features were new. Unlike the original arrangement, which promised to pay claimants 100 cents on the dollar, the new arrangement created a limited pool of assets, whose value is closely tied to the value of the reorganized company and whose distribution is made according to the Trust's ability to pay. The restructuring also replaced the old claims processing method with the "Trust Distribution Process" (TDP). The TDP designates categories of asbestos-related diseases and sets values for each. For example, the standard values for severe asbestosis and lung cancer are $95,000, and the standard value for mesothelioma is $350,000. Once the Trust assigns a disease category, claimants are entitled to a percentage of its value—now only 5 percent—set by the Trust.

The Trust has considerable rulemaking power, and it has used this power to adjust the medical criteria and payout percentages. Disputed claims must go to arbitration, and lawyers' fees are capped at 25 percent of the amounts actually paid to claimants. Under the rules of joint and several liability, claimants can sue others in the chain of distribution for any remaining unpaid damages (and, according to practitioners, claimants often do just that, using proceeds from the Trust to fund additional litigation).

As a technical matter the TDP allows claimants to file tort claims, but effectively it discourages them. First, claimants can file a tort claim only if they select nonbinding arbitration and reject the results. Second, the TDP does not pay punitive damages, even if the claimant wins a tort suit. Third, and most important, if a tort claim exceeds the value of the amount determined through the TDP, that portion of the claim is not paid until all claimants receive 50 percent of the value of their claims—an unlikely prospect, given that current payments are only 5 percent.

By itself, the Manville Trust represents a significant source of asbestos-claim compensation. As of December 31, 2004—a month after the elections that preceded the 109th Congress—the Trust had settled almost 640,000 claims and distributed more than $3.4 billion. The Trust, of course, does not stand alone. By the time Congress considered asbestos litigation reform legislation following the 2004 elections, more than seventy companies with asbestos exposure had filed for Chapter 11 reorganization (see table 2.3 for a summary). As the Manville Trust has done, these trusts have resolved hundreds of thousands of claims and distributed billions of dollars (White 2002). (It should be added that these filings have continued following Congress's failure to act, as Garlock Sealing Technologies, ASARCO LLC, Leslie Controls, Bondex International Inc., Hercules Chemical Company, and others have been added to the list of asbestos-related bankruptcies in the United States.)

Table 2.3.   Companies Filing Asbestos-Related Chapter 11 Reorganizations following Johns-Manville, as of January 1, 2005

2004

- Flintkote
- Pfizer/Quigley

2003

- CE Thurston
- Combustion Engineering
- Congoleum
- Muralo

2002

- A-Best
- AC&S
- A. P. Green
- ARTRA (Synkoloid)
- Harbison Walker
- JT Thorpe
- Kaiser Aluminum and Chemical
- North American Refactories (NARCO)/ RHI
- Plibrico
- Porter Hayden
- Shook & Fletcher
- Western MacArthur

2001

- Bethlehem Steel
- Eastco Industrial Safety Corporation
- Federal Mogul
- G-I Holdings
- Skinner Engine Company
- Swan Transportation
- US Gypsum

2001 (continued)

- US Mineral
- Washington Group International
- W. R. Grace

2000

- Armstrong World Industries
- Babcock & Wilcox
- Burns & Roe Enterprises
- E. J. Bartells
- Owens Corning Fiberglass
- Pittsburgh Corning
- Stone and Webster

1999

- Harnischfeger Industries
- Rutland Fire & Clay

1998

- Atlas Corporation
- Fuller-Austin Insulation
- M. H. Detrick

1996

- Rock Wool Manufacturing

1995

- Lykes Brothers Steamship

1993

- American Ship Building
- Keene Corp.

1992

- Cassiar Mines
- Kentile Floors

1991

- Eagle Picher Industries
- HK Porter Co.

1990

- Celotex
- National Gypsum

1989

- Delaware Insulations
- Hillsborough Holdings
- Lone Star Steel
- Raytech Corporation

1987

- Gatke Corp.
- Nicolet
- Todd Shipyards

1986

- Pacor
- Prudential Lines
- Standard Insulations Inc.
- United States Lines

1985

- Forty-Eight Insulations

1984

- Wallace & Gale

1983

- H&A Construction
- Waterman Steamship Corp.

1982

- Amatex
- UNR Industries

Source: Barnes 2007b.

It is easy to get lost in the details of these plans. The essential institutional point is that these Chapter 11 trusts have added a fundamentally different remedy to the mix of institutional responses to asbestos injury compensation issues. Indeed, these trusts look nothing like traditional tort law or even workers' compensation programs (see table 2.4). Tort law features judges and juries; Chapter 11 trusts do not. Tort law allows for punitive damages; these trusts typically do not. Tort liability is determined by the application of general common-law principles to the merits of individual cases. Trust payments are calculated on the basis of detailed medical criteria and benefit schedules that apply across the board. Tort claims are due in full upon adjudication. Disbursements from these trusts, which are often insolvent, depend on the availability of assets.

The differences between workers' compensation programs and the trusts are less stark because both establish no-fault schemes that categorize claims according to medical criteria and payment schedules. But they still differ significantly as to who decides, who pays, how much, and to whom. Workers' compensation programs are social insurance schemes; public administrators adjudicate claims subject to judicial review. Chapter 11 trusts are private. Private administrators make the key decisions. Workers' compensation programs mandate employer participation, pool costs and risks across companies, and ensure that workers receive full payment of their claims. The trusts are limited funds. They are financed by an equity stake in a single company and thus do not pool risks and costs. Payments are made subject to the availability of trust assets and, in most cases, offer claimants only partial compensation. Finally, workers' compensation programs are limited to workplace injuries; the trusts are not. According to RAND, these court-based tort reforms and parallel private settlement strategies that have consolidated huge numbers of claims have had a profound effect on asbestos injury compensation, rendering the common-law ideal of "individualized process a myth" (Carroll et al. 2002, 129; 2005).

The critical policy point is that fragmentary judicial innovation has not been a substitute for comprehensive legislative action. Instead it has offered decidedly mixed results. Consider the Chapter 11 trusts, which one leading expert described as providing neither "happy nor efficient" results.[13] On one hand, Chapter 11 trusts have saved *individual* companies transaction costs. The administrative costs of the Manville Trust, the largest and longest-running Chapter 11 trust, are about 5 percent of the total dollars spent on claims (Austern 2001). Assuming that attorneys limit themselves to 25 percent, as required by the Trust, plaintiffs receive 70 cents of the total dollars spent as compared with only about 40 cents in ordinary litigation. In

Table 2.4. Summary of the Institutional Effects of Chapter 11 Trusts in the Case of Asbestos

Dimension of Change	Workers' Compensation	Judicial Conversion (Tort Suits)	Judicial Layering (Chapter 11 Trusts)
Who decides?	Public administrators (subject to judicial review)	Judges and juries	Private administrators
Who pays?	Social insurance programs (funded by state-mandated employer premiums)	Wrongdoers (and private insurers)	Chapter 11 trusts (funded by an equity stake in the reorganized company)
How much?	Benefits based on medical costs and two-thirds of salary subject to limits and offsets (no punitive damages)	Damages based on open-ended rules (punitive damages allowed)	Payments based on medical criteria and payment schedules subject to trust liquidity (no punitive damages)
To whom?	Claimants injured at work	Plaintiffs who establish liability, causation, and damages	Claimants meeting exposure criteria

Source: Barnes 2008.

addition, once established, Chapter 11 trusts seem to reduce the time from filing a claim to payment when compared with tort suits (Peterson 1990). As of 2003 the average waiting time under the Manville Trust was about four months.

On the other hand, it is unclear whether these individual savings translate to overall savings or whether litigation costs are merely shifted as new defendants are dragged into court. The reason is that Chapter 11 trusts create limited funds that pay according to the trusts' liquidity, as opposed to the merits of the claims. Under these terms, payments have plummeted in some cases. In the Manville Trust, payments have dropped from 100 percent of liquidated value to 10 percent and now 5 percent. Whether claimants will receive more hinges on their ability to find alternative "deep pockets" under the rules of joint and several liability (or other theories), which allow plaintiffs to sue any company in the chain of distribution for the full amount of damages, or some other theory. The net effect is that the cost of litigation and risk of insolvency falls to either (1) claimants who cannot find other solvent defendants in the supply chain or (2) nonbankrupt companies in the supply chain—many of which had nothing to do with the original concealment of asbestos-related risks. In addition, although Chapter 11 trusts may offer more consistent payments than individual tort suits, they do not ensure uniform payment. Trust terms and liquidity vary over time and across companies, so similar claims are not always treated the same over time or across trusts (Coffee 1995). Under these conditions, Chapter 11 trusts have not only failed to provide fair compensation and contain asbestos-related claims; they have helped spread asbestos litigation. As a result, the more individual defendants have used Chapter 11 to manage their liability, the more entrepreneurial trial lawyers have sought new targets for lawsuits by reaching ever deeper into the chain of distribution, which stretches across thousands of businesses in the case of asbestos.

THE ASBESTOS CRISIS IN THE UNITED STATES

In sum, the asbestos crisis in the United States is not a single, well-contained problem of the past but a cluster of continuing problems that are tightly bundled together. At the most basic level, it is a health crisis that affects millions of ordinary Americans and continues to threaten the public, because millions of tons of asbestos lie in our cars, homes, parks, schools, and office buildings. It should be added that this health crisis is not confined to the United States; it is a global problem (Bowker 2003; Tweedale 2000; see also Banaiie et al. 2000; Kjaergaard and Andersson 2000; Magnani et al. 2000; Peto et al. 1999). The World Health Organization (2006) recently reported that asbestos is responsible for at least 90,000 deaths annually worldwide and that the burden of asbestos-related diseases continues to rise, even in countries that banned its use in the early 1990s.

At another level, the asbestos crisis is an institutional crisis that features a terribly inefficient and unfair response to a major health policy issue. Partly these failures involve a litigation crisis. Although the courts and litigation initially served beneficial policy functions, today's asbestos litigation represents many of the worst aspects of the American tort system (see Kagan 2001). It fails to provide reliable and efficient compensation to the victims of asbestos-related illnesses, while exposing businesses that had little to do with the concealing of the dangers of asbestos to massive costs and uncertainty (see Carrington 2007; Carroll et al. 2002, 2005; Schuck 1992; Huber 1991). Even worse, asbestos litigation has become riddled with questionable and even fraudulent claiming practices that displace consideration of those suffering the most and unfairly burden business (see Koniak 1995, *Mealey's Litigation Report: Asbestos Bankruptcy* 2005; Coffee 1995).

It would be a mistake, however, to lay all the blame on the courts. Judges have not jealously guarded their policymaking turf in the case of asbestos or remained wedded to traditional forms of adjudication in dealing with asbestos-related claims. They have repeatedly tried to use the tools at their disposal to implement a wide range of court-based tort reforms. They have also been candid about the limits of their efforts to address the asbestos crisis and have been asking for legislative relief for years (Barnes 2009a). Congress, meanwhile, has repeatedly failed to heed judicial calls for a federal legislative response to this national health policy disaster. Congressional inertia on this issue is particularly troublesome because, unlike so many policy areas where there is a lack of basic data on the functioning of existing programs, decades of careful studies have demonstrated the excessive costs and inefficiency of the status quo. Thus there is every reason to believe that the nation's leaders should be able to use the politics of efficiency to build a successful reform coalition in Congress. Indeed, as discussed in the next chapter, it is hard to imagine a theoretically better case for using the politics of efficiency to enact meaningful legislation.

NOTES

1. One obvious omission from this book is asbestos abatement issues, such as the removal of asbestos from schools and other public buildings that became a major political issue in the 1980s (see generally, US House of Representatives 1986; Ausness 1994; Connaught 1989; Bureau of National Affairs 1987). It is hoped that what is lost in breadth will be gained in depth, as the analysis focuses on the theoretical lessons that flow from recent attempts of Congress to address asbestos injury compensation issues.

2. "Asbestos" typically refers to six types of natural mineral fibers that have been used commercially: chrysotile (from the mineral group of serpentine) and anthophyllite asbestos, grunerite asbestos (amosite), riebeckite asbestos (crocidolite), tremolite asbestos, and actinolite asbestos (all from the amphibole mineral group). The industrial applications of asbestos have now shifted almost entirely to chrysotile (Virta 2003).

3. The pleura are the membranes that line chest wall and covers the lungs.

4. The latest, serious effort to ban the use of asbestos in the United States (S 742) was introduced by Senator Murray (D-WA). It passed the Senate in 2007 but died in the House of Representatives.

5. This condensed account of the Borel trial is drawn largely from *Borel v. Fibreboard Paper Products Corporation et al.*; Paul Brodeur's *Outrageous Misconduct: The Asbestos Industry on Trial* (Brodeur 1986); and Donald Gifford's *Suing the Tobacco and Lead Pigment Industries* (Gifford 2010).

6. *Restatement of the Law of Tort, Second Edition* (St. Paul: American Law Institute, 1975), §402A.

7. Borel's case was filed in federal court under "diversity jurisdiction," which allows federal courts to hear cases under state law that involve parties from multiple states and involve a threshold amount of damages. This is how the federal courts came to interpret Texas's version of Section 402A.

8. Ward Stephenson himself died of cancer on September 7, 1993, three days before the Fifth Circuit officially handed down *Borel*. Fortunately, Stephenson reportedly heard of his victory through the grapevine before passing away (Brodeur 1986, 67).

9. In the mid-1980s, about a decade after *Borel* and after plaintiff lawyers had uncovered evidence of deliberate concealment of the dangers of asbestos, several state court decisions abandoned the state of the art defense (*Beshada v. Johns-Manville Products Corp.*; *Elmore v. Owens-Illinois, Inc.*).

10. Interview with the author, August 5, 2004.

11. It should be stressed that the treatment here is not exhaustive, because it could easily encompass other examples, including class action lawsuits, group settlements, and the creation of defense consortiums, such as the Asbestos Claims Facility or the Center for Claims Resolution (see Hensler et al. 2000; Coffee 1995; Peterson 1990; Fitzpatrick 1990). Instead, the examples discussed in the text are

intended to illustrate the breadth of court-based tort reforms, which run the gamut from discouragement to replacement.

12. During the middle to late 1990s, class actions seemed poised to become a central tool for implementing court-based replacement reform, promising a means to create private trusts without the costs of bankruptcy, but the Supreme Court pulled the plug on this technique in a series of decisions, including *Amchem Products, Inc. et al. v. George Windsor et al.* and *Ortiz et al. v. Fibreboard et al.* (see Hensler 2002).

13. Interview with the author, March 26, 2006.

Part II

The Case Study

CHAPTER 3

Asbestos Litigation Reform as a "Likely" Case for the Politics of Efficiency

S tudying political dynamics through the lens of the fate of any single legislative proposal, even a substantively important one, raises thorny methodological issues because success and failure in Washington are overdetermined—many factors are relevant, and each might suffice to cause the outcome. At the same time, analyzing cases where our theoretical understanding indicates promising circumstances but failure emerges can be analytically useful. It can probe the boundaries of existing theory, reveal dynamics obscured in ordinary cases, and generate hypotheses that can be tested using other methods as data accumulate (Bennett 2010; Gerring 2004, 2007; see also Collier 1993; Skocpol and Somers 1980; Lijphart 1971; appendix A).

Asbestos litigation reform during the 109th Congress—the congressional session following the 2004 election—fits this profile nicely. First, as Burke (2002) persuasively argues, different types of civil litigation engender different types of politics. The central reform proposal in the 109th Congress—the Fairness in Asbestos Injury Compensation Act, or FAIR Act (S 825)—was a classic replacement reform, which proposed supplanting the court-based system of asbestos injury compensation with a $140 billion federal trust fund that would compensate claimants according to specific medical criteria and cap attorneys' fees at 5 percent. Similar to earlier efforts to enact federal replacement reforms, advocates relied heavily on the politics of efficiency by repeatedly arguing that the existing system was "broken" and seeking to build broad coalitions between plaintiffs' and defendants' groups on the grounds that the new administrative remedy would streamline the adjudication process, replace open-ended legal rules and widely variable jury verdicts with more predictable regulations and administrative procedures, and remove lawyers as intermediaries.

Second, the politics of efficiency seemed poised for success at the outset of the 109th Congress, at least from the perspective of the academic literature. As noted in chapter 1, the literature identifies a series of factors that should set the stage for building winning coalitions that can overcome expected opposition to tort reform from trial lawyers who predictably resist any attempt to lessen the flow of litigation that provides their meal ticket. These factors, again, are (1) support from strategically placed policy entrepreneurs, (2) Republican majorities, (3) bipartisan support, (4) judicial calls for legislation; (5) high legal costs and legal uncertainty; and (6) an expert consensus on the lack of secondary policy benefits of litigation (see Burke 2002; Hausegger and Baum 1999; Ignagni and Meernik 1994; Campbell, Kessler, and Shepherd 1995; Elliott and Talarico 1991; Epstein 1988; O'Connell 1979; see also Esterling 2004; Patashnik 2000; Steinmo and Watts 1995). As detailed below, *all* were present during the 109th Congress. See table 3.1 for a summary.

Support from Strategically Placed Policy Entrepreneurs

The fragmented federal lawmaking process is notoriously complex and difficult to navigate (Morone 1990; Steinmo 1994; Steinmo and Watts 1995; Oberlander 2003a, 2003b). Strategically placed policy entrepreneurs are typically crucial in negotiating this obstacle course and enacting significant civil litigation reforms (Burke 2002). From the start of the 109th Congress, asbestos litigation reform enjoyed support from key policymakers within the Senate, where the central battles over asbestos litigation

Table 3.1. Asbestos Litigation Reform as a "Likely" Case

Factor Favoring Success	Present following the 2004 Election?
Support from strategically located policy entrepreneurs	Yes
Republican majorities	Yes
Bipartisan support	Yes
Judicial calls for legislative action	Yes
High transaction costs and legal uncertainty	Yes
Consensus on lack of secondary policy benefits of tort	Yes

reform were waged during the 109th Congress (Stern 2004a, 2005). Most important, Senator Arlen Specter (R-PA), the chair of the Judiciary Committee and thus the point man for asbestos litigation reform in the Senate, was deeply committed to reform and worked assiduously to pass it. Specter, moreover, was not alone. Other prominent supporters included Senator Patrick Leahy (D-VT), the ranking Democrat on the Judiciary Committee, and Senator Bill Frist (R-TN), the Senate majority leader, who had dubbed asbestos litigation reform a "personal priority" (Perine 2004) and vowed to bring any bill that emerged from the Judiciary Committee promptly to the floor.

Republican Majorities

Studies suggest that Republicans are generally more receptive to civil litigation reform than are Democrats (Burke 2002; Campbell, Kessler, and Shepherd 1995; Elliott and Talarico 1991). The 2004 elections returned a Republican to the White House and increased Republican majorities in both chambers of Congress, as Republicans claimed 231 seats in the House and 55 seats in the Senate. At a minimum, these electoral gains ensured Republican control over the presidency's "bully pulpit" and relevant congressional committees, which are significant advantages, given the president's ability to set agendas and the committees' ability to frame policy options.

Bipartisan Support

Republican majorities did not give Republican policy entrepreneurs carte blanche on Capitol Hill because, as is typical in the current era, they did not have sixty votes in the Senate. They needed some help from the Democratic Party. Fortunately for reform proponents, several key Democrats pledged their support for asbestos litigation reform at the outset of the 109th Congress, including senators Leahy, Dianne Feinstein (D-CA), and Herb Kohl (D-WI) on the Senate Judiciary Committee. Senator Max Baucus (D-MT) had also publicly stated his support for reform efforts, as long as the bill offered adequate relief to victims of asbestos-related diseases who lived in Libby, Montana. Assuming that Republicans toed the line, the support of four Democrats left reformers only one vote shy of the critical threshold for overcoming the Senate's supermajority procedural requirements.

Judicial Calls for Reform

The literature on interbranch relations finds that Congress is more likely to act when the Supreme Court invites legislative action (see Hausegger and Baum 1999; Ignagni and Meernik 1994). In a similar vein Eric Patashnick (2000) finds that Congress is more likely to create federal compensation trusts when other remedies have been exhausted. As was noted in chapter 2, the Supreme Court had been calling for legislation for more than a decade on the grounds that litigation had run its course. In 1990 a special committee of the Judicial Conference on asbestos litigation found as follows: "The situation has reached critical proportions and is getting worse. . . . Dockets . . . continue to grow; long delays are routine; the same issues are litigated over and over; transaction costs exceed the victims' recovery two to one; exhaustion of assets threatens and distorts the process; and future claimants may lose altogether" (Judicial Conference 1991, 2–3).

Given this state of affairs, the conference called on Congress to create a national asbestos injury compensation system (Judicial Conference 1991, 31). Conservative and liberal Supreme Court Justices reiterated these calls in 1997,[1] in 1999,[2] and again in 2003.[3] Shortly after the 2004 election President George W. Bush seized on these judicial pleas for legislative relief, arguing that "when . . . the Supreme Court says we have a national problem, I think Congress needs to listen" (White House Press Release, January 7, 2005, 3).

High Litigation Costs and Legal Uncertainty

The selling points of lower costs and greater certainty had contributed to the passage of other federal replacement reforms (see Burke 2002, 190–91). In the case of childhood vaccines, for example, a surge in litigation and some large jury verdicts coincided with a hundredfold increase in the cost of vaccines, driving the price of a single dose of the DPT vaccine from 11 cents in 1980 to $11.40 by 1986. Even more troubling, the uncertainty of litigation potentially threatened the supply of childhood vaccines in the United States, as some manufacturers claimed that they could no longer find liability insurance at any price (Burke 2002, 144). Under these circumstances, arguments for replacing costly and unpredictable litigation with a relatively streamlined and predictable administrative program were instrumental in bringing key plaintiff and defendant groups together, which in turn was essential to creating the Vaccine Injury Compensation Program, a no-fault, federally run compensation program.

The opportunity to create a similar plaintiff–defendant coalition was clearly available in the case of asbestos litigation reform. As discussed in the last chapter, administrative costs gobble up more than half of every dollar spent to resolve asbestos claims (Kakalik et al. 1983; Hensler et al. 2001; Carroll et al. 2002, 2005). Defendants, meanwhile, have spent more than $70 billion on asbestos claims (Carroll et al. 2002, 2005), and more than 70 companies have been forced into bankruptcy. These bankruptcies have hurt management and workers, costing more than 400,000 jobs and millions in lost pension values (Stiglitz, Orzag, and Orzag 2002).

Placing an exact dollar amount on the potential savings from replacing asbestos litigation is speculative, but the number is undoubtedly enormous. Under the FAIR Act Congress planned to set aside $140 billion for the asbestos injury trust fund and capped attorneys' fees at 5 percent (Fair Act, Section 104[e]). Assuming that the program's other overhead costs doubled this amount, total administrative costs under the FAIR Act would have been about $14 billion. By contrast RAND estimates that the administrative costs of asbestos litigation still account for more than 50 percent of all its costs, or at least $70 billion (Carroll et al. 2005). Using these numbers the FAIR Act promised to transfer at least $56 billion in savings to claimants and defendants, which approaches the initial costs of the government bail-out of General Motors and Chrysler (King and Terley 2009). This estimate, moreover, excludes other potential sources of significant savings from reducing the uncertainty stemming from asbestos litigation, such as lowering the cost of credit and insurance for businesses facing asbestos liability. Given this amount of money on the table, the business community and organized labor should have had strong reasons to coalesce and support replacement reform under the banner of the politics of efficiency (see Burke 2002).

Consensus on the Lack of Secondary Policy Benefits

The politics of efficiency is largely premised on the argument that replacing the status quo will yield broad policy benefits. Accordingly, if asbestos litigation provides secondary policy benefits that offset its costs and inconsistency, the politics of efficiency might lose some of its luster. Put differently, the question is not simply what asbestos litigation costs but also what are we buying with these costs. If the answer is deterrence, individualized justice, and retribution, then there may be fewer policy reasons for Congress to take on the difficult task of passing major civil litigation reform, despite the inefficiency of litigation as a means of compensation.

Thus, one might argue that the unpredictability of asbestos litigation is a (partial) policy blessing in disguise because it promises to enhance the deterrent value of tort law, thereby forcing companies to become extra vigilant. The assertion that tort law provides a valuable deterrent beyond other factors, such as safety regulations and market pressures, is debatable (Kagan 2001; Sugarman 1989). However, even if one concedes this argument, asbestos litigation has increasingly focused on those defendants who played a relatively minor role in exposing workers to asbestos and covering up its dangers. As a result, experts have argued that the deterrence value of these suits has become attenuated. A recent RAND report made the point as follows: "If business leaders believe that tort outcomes have little to do with their own behavior, then there is no reason for them to shape their behavior so as to minimize tort exposure" (Carroll et al. 2005, 129; see also Hanlon 2006).

Nor does asbestos litigation offer an individualized treatment of claims, which is essential to perceptions of procedural fairness and trust in the legal system (Tyler 1990). As early as the mid-1980s, many asbestos claimants were not given their day in court. After six or more years of asbestos litigation, the state court in San Francisco had completed only 11 percent of asbestos cases. In Massachusetts, the news was worse; the state court had resolved only 10 of 2,141 claims, or less than 1 percent (Hensler et al. 1985, 84–85). Today, many claims are tried en masse or lumped into "inventories" for the purposes of massive group settlements, rendering the ideal of particularized justice in asbestos litigation largely moot (Carroll et al. 2005, 129).

Finally, it is hard to maintain that today's asbestos litigation serves to punish corporate wrongdoers. During the late 1970s some opposed asbestos litigation reform precisely because it promised to bail out companies that had callously exposed their workers and the public to hundreds of tons of asbestos while intentionally concealing its risks. By 2004, however, these original defendants were long gone, leaving in their place a series of undercapitalized private trusts and many businesses that had little to do with mining asbestos or hiding its risks. As Patrick Hanlon (2006, 518), a leading practitioner and now a law professor at the University of California, Berkeley, writes, "In this setting, . . . the careful examination of individual responsibility that is supposed to be the centerpiece of the civil justice system seems weirdly out of place."

In short, following the 2004 elections, congressional deference to the courts had become increasingly untenable as a policy matter, while the prospects for congressional action had become increasingly promising as a political matter from the vantage point of the academic literature. More-over, consistent with the literature, concrete signs of hope did emerge at the outset of the 109th Congress. President George W. Bush, for instance, convened a conference on improving the economy soon after his reelection. In his opening remarks he argued that a "cornerstone of any good program is legal reform" (White House Press Release, December 15, 2004, 1). He added: "I intend to take a legislative package to Congress which says that we expect the House and the Senate to pass meaningful liability reform on asbestos." Several weeks later he dedicated precious presidential time to visit Michigan and moderate a roundtable discussion specifically devoted to asbestos litigation reform, where he vowed to keep it on the "front burner" and expressed confidence that "we can get something done" (White House Press Release, January 7, 2005, 4). Senator Specter echoed this sentiment, reporting that he was "very close" to reaching an agreement on a major reform proposal. Senator Leahy sounded even more optimistic, stating that "I think we are very, very close to a bill" (Higgins 2005).

It might be tempting to dismiss these statements as cheap talk in the afterglow of an election, and it is probably true that President Bush's commitment to reform faded over time. Nevertheless, optimism about reform following the 2004 elections was not limited to politicians' sound bites in the media. Wall Street was also bullish. Stock values of companies with significant asbestos-litigation exposure, such as Armstrong Holdings and Owens Corning, jumped more than 80 percent at the outset of the 109th Congress (Higgins 2005). Other companies enjoyed a similar boost. From April 1, 2004, when the Senate filibustered a major asbestos reform effort in the 108th Congress, to mid-November 2004, following the 2004 elections, the stock prices of three other major asbestos litigation defendants—Owens Illinois, USG Corporation, and W. R. Grace—soared 45, 61, and 300 percent, respectively. The Dow Jones Industrial Average, meanwhile, remained relatively flat, gaining about 1.7 percent. Despite these hopeful signs, no stable plaintiff–defendant coalition emerged, and reform initiatives failed. What happened? The next chapter explores this question by examining the critical votes that thwarted reform along with the divisive interest group politics that surrounded congressional efforts to forge a compromise.

NOTES

1. *Amchem Products, Inc. et al. v. George Windsor et al.*, 521 US 591, 716 (1997).
2. *Ortiz et al. v. Fibreboard et al.*, 527 US 815, 821 (1999).
3. *Norfolk & Western Railway Co. v. Ayers*, 538 US 135, 166 (2003).

CHAPTER 4

The Puzzling Politics of the FAIR Act

The demise of asbestos litigation reform in the 109th Congress culminated a long political process that formally encompassed two very different reform approaches, each of which represented a spill-over from the previous session. (Appendix B provides a rough chronology of events during the 108th and 109th Congresses to help orient the reader.) One bill, the Asbestos Compensation Fairness Act of 2005 or "medical criteria bill" (HR 1957), was a discouragement reform, which sought to reduce the amount of litigation without providing an alternative. In effect it proposed to codify the practice of creating inactive dockets for asbestos lawsuits, which required all asbestos claims to meet detailed medical criteria before proceeding to trial. The FAIR Act was the alternative. It adopted a prototypical replacement strategy, seeking to replace litigation with a no-fault, $140 billion federal trust fund financed by asbestos litigation defendants, which would compensate claimants according to detailed medical categories and payment schedules and capped attorneys' fees.

From the start, the House favored the medical criteria bill, but it faced stiff opposition from both ends of the political spectrum. On the left, labor opposed the medical criteria approach, seeing it as unfairly limiting workers' access to the courts. On the right, some businesses argued that a medical criteria bill did not go far enough, because it did nothing to prevent break-the-bank jury verdicts. The FAIR Act, by contrast, offered something to both these groups. It was consistent with labor's long-standing goals of federalizing workers' compensation issues, but it also promised businesses greater certainty with respect to their asbestos injury liability.

The FAIR Act also enjoyed some momentum from the previous session. As the 108th Congress ended, Senate majority leader Bill Frist (R-TN) and minority leader Tom Daschle (D-SD) took the unusual step of asking federal circuit judge Edward Becker to mediate among the stakeholders after an earlier version of the FAIR Act had been filibustered. Following these mediations, Frist and Daschle continued to exchange proposals. Although these negotiations failed to produce a final compromise, some insiders believed that Frist and Daschle's efforts would place the FAIR Act "on the top of the agenda for the next Congress," especially if the Republican Party solidified its majorities (Stern 2004b, 1630).[1]

They were right. Soon after becoming the chair of the Judicial Committee, Senator Arlen Specter (R-PA) held hearings on the FAIR Act. After months of work he managed a bipartisan thirteen-to-five vote for moving the bill out of committee, picking up support from all the Republican senators and three Democrats—Senators Patrick Leahy (VT), Dianne Feinstein (CA), and Herb Kohl (WI). Observers hailed the committee vote as a "big step," in part because Specter proved he could reach across the aisle without losing the support of conservatives, who many felt were the key to passage (Stern 2005).

Almost immediately, however, opposition emerged (Stern 2006a, 2006b). As a policy matter, the devil was in the details, and the details were devilishly complex. In the end three issues proved particularly vexing: the program's cost, funding, and "leakage," meaning the extent to which defendants would have to pay into the fund and nevertheless face future litigation (Hanlon 2006).[2] Moreover, these issues were intertwined because the trust would dissolve if it ran out of money and all claims would return to the courts. As a result, if Congress failed to estimate the amount of claims, the program's administrative costs, or the availability of funding correctly, the trust would automatically terminate and claims would revert to the courts, presenting business with its worst-case scenario of paying for a program without eliminating the risk of litigation.

Under these circumstances reform advocates had to provide credible, if not convincing, cost and funding estimates. However, asbestos injury compensation costs have a long history of defying the experts and exceeding even the most careful estimates. This uncertainty cast a long shadow over negotiations inside the Washington Beltway, as the Congressional Budget Office's scoring of the FAIR Act stressed the difficulty of assessing its final price tag; a Government Accountability Office report on existing federal compensation trusts, such as the Black Lung Disability Trust Fund, emphasized their long history of cost overruns; and a report by Bates White, a private consultancy recruited by businesses that opposed the FAIR Act, predicted that the trust would dissolve within three years and accumulate a $45 billion debt (Hanlon 2006).

Without a strong policy consensus on the numbers, familiar partisan splits emerged on the proposal. Conservative Republican senators—including John Cornyn (TX), Tom Coburn (OK), and Jon Kyl (AZ), who voted the bill out of committee—began to question its substance, fearing that Congress would be forced to rescue the trust from insolvency at tax-payers' expense and create a permanent fixture in the federal bureaucracy. Meanwhile, liberal Democratic senators—including Edward Kennedy (MA), Russell Feingold (WI), Joseph Biden (DE), Charles Schumer (NY), and Dick Durbin (IL) on the Judiciary Committee—feared that the FAIR Act was overly restrictive, underfunded, and tilted toward big business. Over time, opposition began to harden in both directions (*Inside OSHA* 2005). Long before hurricanes Katrina and Rita blew many initiatives off Congress's agenda and the Senate turned to the confirmation of two Supreme Court justices, Senate minority leader Harry Reid (D-NV) quipped, "If anyone thinks they can bring up the asbestos bill and get it passed, I think we can get them a magic show in Las Vegas" (Knight 2005).

Ignoring these gathering political headwinds (and looking for opportunities to burnish his credentials for a potential presidential campaign), Majority Leader Frist attempted to force the issue by scheduling a floor vote on the FAIR Act in February 2006. Frist's plan was thwarted when the conservative Republican senator John Ensign (NV) brought a budgetary point of order based on a prohibition against legislation authorizing more than $5 billion in spending during any ten-year period starting in 2016. Specter countered that the motion was a non sequitur—the proposed trust was privately funded and would sunset upon insolvency. Thus the bill was formally "off budget" and contemplated no federal spending. But deficit hawks rejoined that if the trust went insolvent, Congress would inevitably step in and save the program using general revenues.

Ensign's motion carried the day. On February 14, 2006, supporters of the FAIR Act fell just short of the sixty votes needed to waive the budgetary point of order. The final tally was fifty-eight to forty-one, but the outcome was ostensibly even closer (see table 4.1 for a summary).[3] Senator Frist voted against the bill at the last minute so that he could bring a motion to reconsider if proponents could find the missing vote. Senator Specter quickly insisted that he could deliver the sixtieth vote because Senator Daniel Inouye (D-HI), who was absent, had indicated that he would consider waiving the budgetary point of order if the Senate revisited the FAIR Act.

Despite this flurry of activity, a closer look at key senators suggests that the FAIR Act had lost momentum. Over time, Senator Specter simply could

Table 4.1.   Roll Call Vote on a Motion to Waive Senator Ensign's
Budgetary Point of Order, Senate Vote 21, February 14, 2006

Party	Yeas/Nays
Republicans[a]	44–11
Democrats[b]	13–30
Independent	1–0
Total	58–41

[a] Senator Frist voted against the waiver (and thus against reform) to preserve the right
to bring a motion to reconsider.
[b] Senator Inouye (D-HI) did not vote on the motion.
Note: A three-fifths majority vote (60) is required to waive the Budget Act and overcome
a budgetary point of order. The FAIR Act was subsequently recommitted to the Judiciary
Committee.

not persuade likely allies to give him the benefit of the doubt, while the
opposition seemed to gain traction daily. The problem was what one
insider called "yes, but" support, in which actors expressed support for
the idea of replacement reform but balked at the details of the FAIR Act.[4]
On the left, for example, Senator Kennedy had expressed sympathy for
Specter's efforts and seemed willing to work with him to create a new
health program for asbestos workers and their families. In the end, however, Kennedy believed that the bill was simply too narrow, because it,
among other things, excluded a category of smokers from the trust fund
provisions. Broadening the bill, however, would have alienated Specter's
likeminded moderate Republican colleagues, such as Senator Judd Gregg
(R-NH), who were also open to passing asbestos litigation reform but
believed that the FAIR Act was already underfunded and that Congress
would eventually be forced to cover its costs.

Meanwhile, conservatives, even the bill's supposed proponents, seemed
increasingly dubious. Critically, senators Coburn, Cornyn, and Kyl
expressed growing hostility. Although they voted the FAIR Act out of
committee and favored waiving Ensign's budgetary point of order, they
made it abundantly clear that if the FAIR Act proceeded to a vote, they
would push a series of major amendments, including one that would substitute the House medical criteria bill for the FAIR Act. Others, like Robert
Bennett (R-UT), remained concerned about the bill's effect on small businesses, because the FAIR Act's formula for calculating contributions was
based on historical rates of asbestos liability that tended to hit smaller firms

harder than large, multinational corporations, such as General Electric and Honeywell. Perhaps even more important, by the time the FAIR Act had stumbled in the Senate, opposition to replacement reform had intensified in the Republican-controlled House, as conservative groups like FreedomWorks, led by former representative Dick Armey (R-TX), publicly excoriated the idea of creating a new federal program, especially one that seemed to earmark $7 billion for trial lawyers (Stern 2006b). In short, the FAIR Act was already caught in heavy crossfire when it fell on Ensign's budgetary point of order. The FAIR Act and the more modest medical criteria bill were never reconsidered. For the second session in a row, the politics of efficiency had fallen short on issues related to asbestos injury compensation.

Digging even deeper, reform advocates not only failed to get the necessary votes in the Senate but also failed to build a broad reform coalition that encompassed a critical mass of plaintiffs' and defendants' groups, which has been crucial to passing other replacement reforms (Burke 2002; see table 4.2 for a summary).[5] On the plaintiff side, victims' groups were deeply split, mostly between the worried well—those who have been exposed to asbestos but are not yet ill, who favored a system that spread compensation among future and present claims—and those who were already ill and were poised to bring lawsuits in search of huge jury verdicts. The labor unions were also fractured. The United Auto Workers and Asbestos Workers Union supported the bill as a step forward, but the AFL-CIO did not support it, which reflected its growing alliance with trial lawyers under John Sweeney, who had become its president in part by opposing his predecessor's willingness to compromise on asbestos injury compensation issues.

With respect to businesses, companies divided mostly along the lines of their potential liability, as companies with large and uncertain liabilities generally supported the FAIR Act while others with more manageable liabilities favored a medical criteria bill. Specifically, some large and influential companies and their representatives—including General Electric, Viacom, the National Association of Manufacturers and the Asbestos Alliance—strongly supported the FAIR Act, arguing that the uncertainty resulting from asbestos litigation was unnecessarily hampering credit and creating a drag on economic activity (Higgins 2005). But other businesses and their representatives—including Exxon-Mobil, Borg Warner, and the Coalition for Asbestos Reform—vigorously opposed the bill. They argued that the FAIR Act was underfunded (and thus would leak) and that its contribution formulas were unfair. Insurance companies divided along

Table 4.2. Public Positions on the FAIR Act

Group	For	Against

Business groups	Asbestos Alliance
	National Association of
	  Manufacturers
	Asbestos Study Group
	National Association of
	  Wholesalers and
	  Distributors
	National Small Business
	  Association
	Small Business and
	  Entrepreneurship Council
	American Small Business
	  Association
	Women Impacting Public
	  Policy
		American Insurance
		  Association
		Coalition for Asbestos Reform
		Common Interest Group
		National Association of Mutual
		  Insurance Companies
		National Industrial Sand
		  Association
		Property Casualty Insurance
		  Association of America

Individual businesses	Armstrong World Industries Dow Ford General Electric General Motors Georgia Pacific Honeywell McDermott Owens Corning Owens-Illinois Pfizer St. Gobain USG Corporation Viacom World Industries WR Grace	Borg Warner Exxon-Mobil Foster Wheeler NSI
Insurance companies	ACE CNA Liberty Mutual	AIG Equitas Gen Re Hartford Liberty Mutual Travelers

Plaintiffs groups	RetireSafe
	Veterans of Foreign Wars
	The Seniors Council
	United Auto Workers
	Asbestos Workers Union
		White Lung Association
		Committee to Protect
		  Mesothelioma Victims
		Asbestos Disease Awareness
		  Organization
		AFL-CIO

Others	Council for Citizens against
	  Waste in Government
	National Legal and Policy
	  Center
	American Medical Association
		Public Citizen
		National Taxpayer Union
		FreedomWorks
		Governor Rick Perry (Texas)

Source: Content analysis by the author, January 2005 to January 2007.

similar lines, with some companies with large liabilities supporting the bill on the grounds that it replaced a hopelessly inefficient system but others opposing it because it was seen as too expensive while offering too little certainty about future claims.

Companies that had filed for bankruptcy were particularly interesting on this front, because their positions seemed to shift over time. In the early 1980s, before most companies had filed for bankruptcy and created their own compensation trusts, Congress held hearings on the need for asbestos litigation reform. As now, companies with high exposure to asbestos litigation, like Pacor, tend to support the creation of a "global solution" to the asbestos crisis (House Committee on Labor Standards 1983, 45). By 2005, however, many of these companies had filed for bankruptcy and exited the tort system, creating a series of Chapter 11 trusts to deal with their remaining liability. In contrast to the companies that created them, these trusts strongly opposed the FAIR Act, arguing that its proposal to use their assets to fund the new federal program was unconstitutional. Put differently, court-based replacement reform not only diverted litigation to the trusts as a legal matter but also seemed to replace the likely allies of reform—high-exposure defendants, such as Pacor—with staunch reform opponents, such as the Chapter 11 trusts, as a political matter.

It did not help the reformers that public interest groups were also at odds. Some, like the National Legal Policy Center, fully embraced the politics of efficiency and the passage of the FAIR Act. It argued that passing replacement reform would "end the circus of runaway asbestos litigation that has amply rewarded a handful of lawyers while leaving thousands of desperately sick people with a fraction of the compensation they deserve. This abuse of the legal system has already driven at least 70 corporations into bankruptcy and jeopardized thousands of American jobs" (*PR Newswire* 2005). Meanwhile, an unlikely alliance between Ralph Nader's Public Citizen and Dick Armey's FreedomWorks attacked the bill from the left and the right, respectively, maintaining that the bill was simultaneously a corporate bailout and a big-government boondoggle.

From a distance these splits are surprising, especially the divisions among and within the plaintiffs' and defendants' groups that could have potentially realized billions in savings through the passage of replacement reform. Thus the real puzzle of the FAIR Act is not that it failed or that trial lawyers—led by the American Association for Justice (AAJ), formerly known as the American Trial Lawyers Association—opposed it. It is always difficult to pass major replacement reform, and trial lawyers typically oppose civil litigation reforms that threaten their livelihood (Burke 2002).

Rather, the mystery is the lack of support among other stakeholders, such as victims and businesses, which collectively bear the brunt of the system's billions of dollars in waste. According to insiders, more than anything else, these splits doomed the FAIR Act in the Senate and made its replacement strategy a nonstarter in the House.

EXPLAINING THE POLITICS OF ASBESTOS LITIGATION REFORM

As noted in chapter 3, it is difficult—if not impossible—to provide a definitive explanation of the failure of any bill in the context of a single case study, because many factors contributed to the downfall of the FAIR Act, and each may have been sufficient to derail the bill by itself. Nevertheless, by tracing several plausible explanations, we can probe their limits and generate hypotheses about the broader politics of efficiency. In this spirit of exploration, the remainder of this chapter looks at the demise of the FAIR Act through four different theoretical lenses: (1) partisan dynamics; (2) "capture" by lawyers; (3) the quality of policy entrepreneurship; and (4) interbranch dynamics, especially how judicial innovation reinforced congressional inertia. Each is discussed in turn.

Partisan Dynamics

The immediate cause of the FAIR Act's demise was the vote that failed to waive Senator Ensign's budgetary point of order. This vote is a textbook illustration of the difficulty of moving to the center without losing votes from the base in an age of ideologically polarized parties (see table 4.3). Specifically, ten Republicans bolted from the majority of their party to vote against the FAIR Act.[6] Statistically, the mean nominate score—Poole and Rosenthal's standard measure of the members' political ideology—for antireform Republicans was significantly to the right of proreform Republicans. Meanwhile, thirty Democratic senators voted against the FAIR Act. Their nominate scores were to the left of the proreform Democrats' scores, although the statistical significance of the difference was weaker. In short, bill proponents held the center but lost the wings of each party, especially the Republicans.

Of course, many factors might shape an individual senator's vote on a given bill, especially a large and complex measure like the FAIR Act. As such, divisions within the Republican delegation surely reflected factors

Table 4.3. Ideological Analysis of Republican and Democratic Proreform and Antireform Factions on the Vote to Waive Senator Ensign's Budgetary Point of Order

Party Faction[a]	Number (% of Delegation)	Mean Nominate Score (Standard Error)	Distance from Proreform Faction
Antireform Republicans	10 (18)	.57 (.04)	.14 to the right**
Proreform Republicans	45 (82)	.43 (.03)	—
Proreform Democrats	13 (30)	−.36 (.03)	—
Antireform Democrats	30 (70)	−.45 (.03)	.09 to the left*

[a] Senator Frist is included in the Republican proreform faction despite his formal vote for reasons explained in the text. Senator Jeffords, as an independent, is excluded from the analysis. Senator Inouye, a Democrat, did not vote on the motion.

* Difference is statistically significant beyond the .10 level.

** Difference is statistically significant beyond the .05 level.

other than ideology, including sincerely held disagreements over policy details (see Hanlon 2006). But a simple roll call analysis of Republican votes on the waiver suggests that ideology did in fact play a significant role in the process. As seen in tables 4.4 and 4.5, after roughly controlling for incumbency, proximity to an election, region, and campaign contributions from the leading trial lawyer advocacy group, the AAJ, ideology was correlated with an antireform vote beyond the .05 level of statistical significance. In the median case, a shift to the right of 1 standard deviation increased the likelihood of an antireform vote among Republicans by 25 percent.[7] These findings suggest that Senator Specter and his allies were simply unable to move to the center while maintaining sufficient support from the right.

This explanation, however, does not go very far in illuminating the politics of efficiency or the underlying interest group politics of the FAIR Act. After all, the challenge of holding the center while reaching out to the base is a generic one; it faces reform proponents regardless of whether they seek to use the politics of efficiency as a strategy for navigating today's challenging legislative environment. Moreover, partisan dynamics among senators lend little insight into the puzzling interest group politics underlying the failure of the FAIR Act. Thus, though partisan tensions may have been a proximate cause of the FAIR Act's failure, we need to look further if we want to learn more about the politics of efficiency and understand the absence of a broad reform coalition in the case of asbestos.

Table 4.4. Roll Call Analysis of Republican Votes on the Waiver of the Budgetary Point of Order, Senate Vote 21, February 14, 2006

Variable	Measure	Expected Effect	Coefficient (Standard Error)
Ideology	Nominate score for 109th Congress	+	7.06** (.3.21)
AAJ contributions	Total dollars given as of February 24, 2006	+	.15** (.07)
Election cycle	2, 4, 6 (6 is an election year)	+	−.51 (.34)
Service years	Years in office (as of February 14, 2006)	−	−.07 (.08)
South	0,1 (no, yes)	+/−	−1.23 (1.36)
East	0,1 (no, yes)	+/−	2.42 (1.59)
West	0,1 (no, yes)	+/−	.64 (1.32)
Constant	—	—	−3.39 (2.36)

** Difference is statistically significant beyond the .05 level.

Note: $N = 56$ (includes Senator Frist). Percent correctly predicted = 85.45. The vote is coded as 1 for nay (with the AAJ position, against reform), 0 for yea (against the AAJ position, proreform).

Table 4.5. First-Difference Effects of Ideology and AAJ Contributions on the Republican Vote in the Median Case

Variable	Median Value	Standard Deviation	From, To	Expected Effect on Vote[a]	First Difference
Ideology (nominate)	.46	.22	(.46, .68)[b]	+	.25
AAJ contributions (thousands)	0	6.29	(0, 6.29)	+	.17

[a] The vote is coded as 1 for nay (in favor of the AAJ position) and 0 for yea (against the AAJ position).
[b] A movement of 1 standard deviation in the positive direction represents 1 standard deviation to the right on the political spectrum.

Capture by Lawyers

An alternative explanation of the failure of the FAIR Act concerns trial lawyers. In the classic formulation, trial lawyers are said to have "captured" the process with the help of Democrats, who receive the bulk of their campaign contributions (see, e.g., Epstein 1988; O'Connell 1979; and, generally, Stigler 1971; Tollison 1982). The gist is that trial lawyers pressure strategically placed Democrats to use veto points in Congress— committees, floor votes, and a wide range of procedural maneuvers, such as filibusters and points of order—to play defense and block reforms.

This argument has some appeal. The AAJ and other trial lawyers vigorously opposed reform, and reform foundered on a supermajority veto point in the Senate. Indeed, trial lawyers not only flexed their political muscles on Capitol Hill by directly lobbying members of Congress but also sought to create pressure on senators from constituents in their home states. For example, Mark Iola, president of the Senate Accountability Project and a plaintiffs' lawyer, sponsored a local television ad against Republican senator Jeff Sessions (AL), which accused the senator of betraying his conservative roots by supporting a "liberal entitlement program that takes power away from ordinary citizens and gives it to bureaucrats in Washington" (Orndorff 2005).

According to the roll call analysis, the trial lawyers' opposition to the bill paid off. As seen in tables 4.4 and 4.5, controlling for other factors, AAJ contributions were correlated with an antireform vote beyond the .05 level and, in the median case, an increase of AAJ contributions by 1 standard deviation to a Republican senator, or about $6,300, increased the likelihood of an antireform vote by 17 percent. This is hardly surprising;

every dollar taken out of the tort system by reform represents a loss to the trial bar, and those receiving AAJ contributions are likely to be sympathetic to trial lawyers' arguments (for both political and policy reasons). As such, the AAJ had every reason to oppose the FAIR Act, which threatened to squeeze the pocketbooks of its members, and it possessed the political wherewithal and connections to fight reform effectively.

It is worth noting, however, that the role of trial lawyers in asbestos litigation reform has been far more complex than is suggested in the literature. Contrary to the classic version of the capture argument, Republicans—not Democrats—brought the procedural motion that killed the FAIR Act. Moreover, a majority of Republicans who torpedoed the FAIR Act (by voting against the waiver of Ensign's point of order) received no campaign contributions from the AAJ. Meanwhile, many staunch Democratic allies of the trial bar, including senators Patrick Leahy and Dianne Feinstein, who had received such contributions, were leading supporters of the bill.

When one steps back from the 109th Congress, the standard capture argument becomes even more problematic. Contrary to the literature's assumption that trial lawyers will always close ranks and oppose reform, plaintiffs' lawyers have had some history of splitting over various reform issues in the asbestos case. Put simply, the complexity of asbestos litigation has resulted in specialization among lawyers, which in turn has shaped their stances on asbestos litigation reform. Lawyers specializing in cancer cases, such as Steve Kazan, opposed a trust fund but had earlier testified in favor of medical criteria reform that would prioritize their clients' claims. Large-inventory lawyers—that is, lawyers who represent large groups of claimants with differing levels of illness—tended to prefer the status quo, because they can obtain higher settlements if they package a few cancer claims with a large number of claims by the worried well. Meanwhile, some prominent lawyers, such as Richard Scruggs, publicly supported the FAIR Act on the grounds that it would rationalize payments and ensure that future claimants would not be shortchanged.

In short, although trial lawyer opposition certainly played a part in defeating the FAIR Act, the traditional capture account of trial lawyers' position on reform seems thin. Those close to the process tended to agree, arguing that AAJ's opposition could have been overcome by a unified front among business groups and victims but that no such coalition emerged. Under these circumstances, the trial lawyers' opposition should be seen as a piece of the puzzle but not necessarily the most important one—a finding that is consistent with other studies on replacement reforms (Burke 2002;

Barnes 1997). Moreover, this lawyer-centric explanation is silent on why other stakeholders failed to join forces, leaving open the critical question of why victims and business interests remained internally divided.

The Quality of Policy Entrepreneurship

The simplest explanation for the absence of a successful reform coalition lies in the quality of leadership on Capitol Hill. Stitching together plaintiff–defendant coalitions in favor of replacement reform is always tricky, requiring skillful policy entrepreneurship and deft maneuvering to bring litigation rivals together in a political coalition, avoid obstacles in Congress, and isolate opposition from the trial bar and small-government conservatives, who would be expected to oppose any attempt to create a new federal program (Burke 2002). Accordingly, it is possible that the lack of effective political leadership doomed the FAIR Act.

Given the Republican majorities in the 109th Congress, the ideal leader in the Senate would have been a passionate reformer who could move to the center without alienating the base of the Republican Party. In retrospect, Specter may have been ill cast for this role. Although he was dedicated to reform and willing to reach across the aisle, he was distrusted by conservatives, who openly opposed his appointment to the chair of the Judiciary Committee at the beginning of the 109th Congress. This opposition was not without reason. Before he defected to the Democratic Party, Specter was the most liberal Republican on the Senate Judiciary Committee based on his performance during the previous session (fig. 4.1).

In addition, core constituencies within the Republican Party had specific grievances against Specter. Because he was one of the few Senate Republicans who favored abortion rights, social conservatives never trusted him. He managed to antagonize this group on the eve of the 2004 elections, stating that "when you talk about judges who would change the right of a woman to choose, overturn *Roe v. Wade*, I think that is unlikely" (Perine 2004). Richard Land, head of the Southern Baptist Convention, the largest Protestant denomination in the United States, retorted, "Either he gets with the program or we shove him aside" (Cochran 2004). It was perhaps less widely noted that some fiscal conservatives also had misgivings. For example, the National Taxpayers Union, an antitax group, sought to block Specter's rise to the Judiciary Committee chair, in part because they feared he would block discouragement reforms aimed at deterring tort litigation.

These concerns proved prescient. Specter's first critical decision was to focus on the FAIR Act at the exclusion of the medical criteria bill and its

Figure 4.1. Ideology of Senate Judiciary Committee Members: 108th Congress

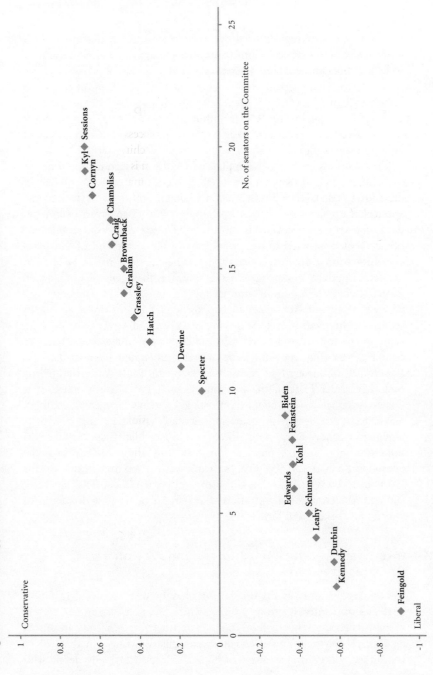

Source: Compiled by the author from Poole and Rosenthal 2007.

discouragement strategy favored by conservatives. Given this choice, it is hardly surprising that defections from the right appeared almost immediately after Specter brokered a bipartisan deal to report the FAIR Act out of committee, as conservative members of the Judiciary Committee quickly distanced themselves from the bill as it moved toward a vote on the floor. Pushing this argument to its logical limit suggests a central irony: A more conservative senator may have been better positioned to move to the center on asbestos litigation reform.

Although this story may seem plausible in the abstract, it should not be overstated. After all, Senator Orrin Hatch (R-UT), the previous chair of the Senate Judiciary Committee, who is slightly more conservative than Specter (recall figure 4.1), failed to build a winning coalition in favor of the FAIR Act's predecessor, as did the even more conservative Majority Leader Frist, who tried to negotiate his own bill at the end of the 108th Congress. Moreover, interviewees close to negotiations in the Senate did not fault Specter's leadership. To the contrary, they generally applauded his skill and determination, noting that (1) he had little choice but to promote the FAIR Act, given the opposition of key business and labor groups to the medical criteria approach; (2) he did a remarkable job in gaining bipartisan support out of the Judiciary Committee; and (3) a more conservative senator would have probably alienated Democrats, who already had filibustered an earlier version of the FAIR Act promoted by Majority Leader Frist in the previous session. From this vantage, it is unclear whether *anyone* could have cobbled together a winning coalition for the FAIR Act, despite the ostensibly favorable conditions for the politics of efficiency. Moreover, even if Specter could have built a successful coalition with more nimble political footwork, this argument still begs the question of why nimble political footwork was needed to gain support for legislation aimed at reducing the prevailing system's demonstrable cost and unpredictability and, in effect, transferring billions of dollars from lawyers to workers and businesses.

Interbranch Relations: Judicial Innovation and Congressional Inertia

A final explanation centers on the interplay between evolving litigation strategies and interest group politics, which is often overlooked by the literature because scholars tend to focus narrowly on either congressional or judicial activities. This oversight is particularly suspect in the case of civil litigation reform, because courts and litigation formally define who pays, how much, and to whom. These decisions, in turn, naturally shape stakeholders' interests in the reform process. In fact, divisions that may seem odd at first glance make perfect sense once one understands how evolving legal standards and litigation practices have shaped the interests of various stakeholder groups (Barnes 2007b; see also Epstein 1988).

Consider victims. As noted above, attorneys have developed different strategies for different types of claims over time. Under these circumstances plaintiff groups now have very different stances on reform. Victims with cancers and other serious illnesses tend to do well in jury trials and typically oppose a national trust fund that would cut off access to the courts. The worried well, those who have been exposed to asbestos but have not yet fallen ill, are generally more receptive to the creation of a central program that would spread compensation among present claims and their own claims that will ripen in the future.

A similar analysis applies to asbestos litigation defendants, whose material interests and thus their positions on asbestos litigation reform have been deeply shaped by judicial innovations (Barnes 2007b). Examples abound; a few should suffice. The most straightforward illustration concerns judicial interpretations of legal liability rules. All things being equal, as liability rules are construed broadly, the targets of litigation should have a stake in seeking legislation that curbs or eliminates lawsuits. However, litigation risks rarely fall evenly on individual businesses and insurance companies. Some business sectors are exposed; others are not. Within business sectors that face a potential wave of litigation, some businesses are better positioned to absorb litigation costs because they are bigger, better insured, and/or have stronger legal defenses. Similarly, insurance companies' exposure to litigation risks varies depending on their underlying contractual obligations, portfolio of policyholders, and reinsurance policies.

In the case of asbestos, the courts generated massive liability risks for businesses and their insurance companies when they endorsed strict liability under *Borel* and its progeny and interpreted general-liability insurance policies broadly in cases like *INA v. Forty-Eight Insulation, Inc.*, and *Keene Corp. v. INA*.[8] Given this spike in potential legal risks, one might expect asbestos defendants and their insurance companies to rally to the cause of reform. However, these risks were unevenly distributed (see Leone 1986; Melnick 1998). As a result, asbestos defendants roughly divided between those with higher exposure, who generally favored replacement reform, and those with less exposure, who generally favored a medical criteria approach or no bill at all. Moreover, as rules switched and reduced immediate risks for particular defendants, they often switched sides. This makes

sense. Why should defendants with lower exposure to litigation risks support legislation that benefits their competitors with higher risks?

Judicial innovations have shaped the interest group politics of asbestos
litigation reform in other, subtler ways. In general, one tends to think of the
courts as the interpreters of law and not the creators of new administrative
mechanisms. However, as explained in chapter 2, the courts have proven
remarkably resourceful in implementing piecemeal court-based replacement reforms: the use of existing rules and procedures, such as Chapter 11
reorganization, to establish privately funded, independently administered
compensation funds on a company-by-company basis (see Barnes 2007b).
Politically, the layering of Chapter 11 trusts on top of the already-complex
mix of remedies contributed to the downfall of the FAIR Act by adding an
additional set of active reform opponents into the process. Specifically, the
Chapter 11 trusts represent distinct entities that control billions of dollars
in assets. One would expect such entities to engender strong support coalitions, and this is exactly what happened. As noted above, in the fight over
the FAIR Act, the trusts and their lead lobbyist, former senator Don Nickles
(R-OK), strongly fought to protect these trusts and their assets; they
demanded that the FAIR Act allow them to opt out of the program entirely
and vowed to challenge the constitutionality of any bill that threatened to
raid their assets to fund a federal compensation program (Stern 2006a,
2006b).

According to some observers, the opposition of the Chapter 11 trusts
provided a double blow to the FAIR Act (Stern 2006a, 2006b; see also
Nagareda 2007). On one hand, the emergence of the trusts further fragmented an already-divided group of business interests, replacing reform
allies like Pacor with reform opponents like the Chapter 11 trusts. On the
other hand, proponents of the FAIR Act were counting on Chapter 11 trust
assets to partially fund the FAIR Act during its crucial start-up period, when
experts expected a rush of claims. The determination of these defendants to
challenge the use of their trust assets in court only reinforced concerns
about the trust's liquidity and ability to contain asbestos litigation risks.

SUMMING UP

The FAIR Act had a seemingly promising legislative start following the
2004 elections, but its prospects quickly faded in the Senate, because reform
proponents could not muster the necessary sixty votes to waive Senator
Ensign's budgetary point of order. A variety of factors surely contributed

to the demise of the FAIR Act: partisan dynamics in an age of narrow majorities and ideological polarized parties; well-organized trial lawyers' opposition; the quality of leadership inside the Senate; and the interplay between judicial innovation and congressional inertia, especially the emergence of court-based tort reforms like the Chapter 11 trusts.

Probably the best explanation incorporates each of these factors and stresses their interrelationship. Thus, it is always difficult to pass major legislative reform, especially in an age of intense partisan rivalries, party polarization, and an increased use of supermajority procedural hurdles in the Senate. The emergence of court-based tort reforms and related judicial innovations served to complicate this already-difficult task by hindering efforts to build a broad reform coalition in Washington on replacement reform on several fronts. They fragmented stakeholder groups, created new interests that benefitted from these arrangements, and provided partial exit strategies for some groups, which reduced the sense of urgency for comprehensive reform. In this challenging political setting and tangled interest group environment, even a dedicated and skillful policy entrepreneur such as Senator Specter, could not navigate the obstacles of determined opposition, narrow majorities, divided parties, and points of order in the Senate. The tragic result is that the current system grinds on to the collective detriment of victims and businesses, even if some individual groups have done well under the existing arrangements.

This failure raises a series of broader questions: What does it teach about the usefulness of the politics of efficiency as a legislative strategy? What does it say about the prospects for institutional reform in an age of polarized parties, narrow majorities, and supermajority requirements in the Senate? And looking ahead to future studies, how should we grapple with the enormous complexity underlying today's policymaking? Part III addresses these issues in two installments. First, it looks at the lessons of the case for the politics of efficiency as a coalition-building strategy. Second, it considers the implications of the case for the US system's capacity for institutional change, the role of the courts in contemporary American policymaking, and the methods for conducting other studies of policymaking.

NOTES

1. According to several insiders who were interviewed for this project, Daschle offered only tepid support for the FAIR Act and may have even been an obstacle to reform. If so, his ouster during the 2004 elections was another political factor favoring action during the 109th Congress.

2. Going into the negotiations, there was particular concern about the treatment of those who showed signs of exposure but whose health remained unimpaired. In that event, a consensus emerged that the worried well would receive compensation only for the costs of medical monitoring and nothing more.

3. It is notoriously difficult to interpret roll call votes. The final vote on the waiver may, in fact, not have been as close as it seemed. One possibility is that some senators voted in favor of the waiver knowing that it would fail in order to gain favor with the supporters of the FAIR Act, which included a number of senior members in leadership positions, including Majority Leader Frist. However, none of the interviewees for this project indicated that this was the case. To the contrary, they indicated that there was sincere support for the bill on both sides of the aisle.

4. Comments during asbestos conference in Northern California, February 10, 2004.

5. To generate this content analysis we searched several publications including *CQ Weekly*, the *New York Times*, the *Philadelphia Inquirer*, the *Washington Post*, the *Wall Street Journal*, and the *National Journal* in addition to the LexisNexis database for all major newspapers from January 2005 to January 2007. We searched using the terms "asbestos," "Congress," FAIR Act," "FAIR," and "fairness in asbestos injury resolution." In combing through these articles, we looked for reported support and opposition for the FAIR Act and cross-referenced these groups with their organizational websites. As a check on validity, we circulated the results to lobbyists who were familiar with the negotiations. Despite our best efforts, a few caveats are worth noting. First, the goal of the exercise was very modest. We were not trying to establish the universe of positions among all stakeholders or the intensity of their preferences but only that there were conflicting views on the FAIR Act among various stakeholder groups. Thus, even if some disagreement may exist about particular entries in the table, there is little disagreement that the FAIR Act was divisive or that divisions existed within and across stakeholder groups. Second, some of the groups were described as fronts for individual interests and, as such, there may be some double counting in the table. The key point, however, remains: despite the promised benefits of reform, interest groups remained remarkably divided on asbestos litigation reform.

6. This number excludes Frist, who publicly supported the FAIR Act but voted against waiving Ensign's point of order for purely procedural reasons, giving him the option of bringing a motion to reconsider. Given Senator Frist's public commitment to asbestos litigation reform and comments of insiders, there is little reason to doubt his sincerity. I have not included Senator Inouye because his position was

far more speculative; however, inclusion of his vote would not significantly change any of the statistical analyses of the vote.

7. Significance was also tested using nested models and likelihood-ratios χ^2, which are more definitive than asymptotic z tests. The results were nearly identical. In fact, ideology was even more statistically significant using these measures.

8. In these insurance cases, asbestos defendants argued that asbestos exposure represented a "continuing tort," meaning that all the insurers that covered the company during the period of exposure were "on the risk" and thus were responsible for defending the suits arising from the exposure and indemnifying the insured company for any payments to the claimants. Insurance companies rejoined that coverage was triggered only when claimants knew or should have known they were suffering from asbestos-related diseases, meaning that companies that had issued older policies would be "off the risk." The courts sided with the defendants and endorsed the "exposure theory" on the grounds that insurance policies should be construed broadly in the case of ambiguity (see, generally, Brodeur 1986).

Part III

Implications

CHAPTER 5

The Asbestos Case and the Politics of Efficiency

The politics of efficiency is not limited to the case of asbestos. It has been a recurring theme during the Barack Obama administration. In his inaugural address, President Obama challenged the nation to "set aside childish things" and squarely confront the "gathering clouds and raging storms" of wars abroad, a faltering economy, a dysfunctional health care system, broken schools, and an outdated infrastructure whose dependence on oil simultaneously strengthens our enemies and threatens our planet. To meet these daunting tasks, Obama urged us to look beyond the "stale political arguments" of the past that "for too long have strangled our politics." The key, he argued, was asking not "whether our government is too big or too small, but whether it works." The administration sounded similar themes throughout the debate on health care and financial market reform, stating that "our test is, what is going to work?" (Puzzanghera 2009). Obama returned to the politics of efficiency in his 2011 state of the union address by pressing Democrats and Republicans to make government "more efficient" by "getting rid of waste."

The politics of efficiency is also not limited to contemporary policy debates. As noted in the introduction, at least as far back as the Progressive Era, reformers have focused on "what works" in trying to overcome entrenched partisan politics, as Progressives would claim that there was no such thing as Republican or Democratic roads, just good or bad ones. The politics of efficiency were equally prominent during the debates over deregulation in the 1980s. In that case reformers maintained that reduced regulation would expose inefficient regulated industries to market competition, which would create better services and lower prices for consumers (Derthick and Quirk 1985). The implication was that if policymakers provided the conditions necessary for greater market efficiency, the politics would fall into place because the promise of improved performance would benefit enough of the relevant interests to overcome industry's resistance to change.

The use of the politics of efficiency in diverse historical and policy settings attests to its broad appeal. Indeed, in the abstract, its logic seems almost irresistible. As noted in the introduction, there are no natural partisan differences over making existing policies and institutional arrangements run more smoothly. In a time of soaring budget deficits, Democrats and Republicans should be drawn to delivering the same benefits for less. As a result, the politics of efficiency seems to be a promising path for sidestepping the political thicket of polarized parties, narrow majorities, and supermajority procedural requirements in the Senate.

Of course, logic and political effectiveness do not always go together in Washington. Accordingly, this book has examined the use of the politics of efficiency in promoting asbestos litigation reform. It has argued that the case of asbestos provides an interesting vantage point from which to view the promise and limits of the politics of efficiency, because there was a broad consensus that asbestos litigation is highly inefficient and policy entrepreneurs leaned heavily on efficiency arguments in trying to sell the FAIR Act in the Senate. The argument is not that the asbestos case is typical (White 2004). As with any single case, the asbestos story has its share of idiosyncrasies and context-specific features. Nevertheless, the asbestos story is a theoretically interesting case because the literature suggests that the politics of efficiency seemed likely to succeed yet it failed. Under these circumstances the asbestos case, like an engineer's stress test, can reveal insights about institutional dynamics that may be missed in routine cases and help probe the analytical boundaries of existing theory. With these goals in mind this chapter considers what went right and wrong for the politics of efficiency in the case of asbestos, with an emphasis on identifying factors that are likely to recur and shape other cases.

WHAT WENT RIGHT FOR THE POLITICS OF EFFICIENCY IN THE ASBESTOS CASE?

It is easy to focus on the failure of asbestos litigation reform in the 109th Congress and to assume that the politics of efficiency has no place in today's challenging legislative environment. That would be a mistake. The first lesson of the case of asbestos is not that the politics of efficiency is ineffective; it is that the politics of efficiency can engender significant—although not necessarily sufficient—bipartisan support for major reform on controversial issues, despite the poisonous partisan environment in Washington.

Recall the critical vote on the FAIR Act in the Senate, the vote to waive the budgetary point of order brought by fiscal conservatives. In that vote the politics of efficiency helped to produce support from fifty-nine senators, only one short of the critical threshold of sixty votes.[1] This group included forty-five Republicans, thirteen Democrats, and one independent, who represented thirty-six states from every region in the nation—the North, South, Midwest, Southwest, and West (see table 5.1). They also occupied an impressive ideological spectrum that held the center, garnering support from moderates of both parties—such as Republican senators Lincoln Chafee of Rhode Island and Olympia Snowe of Maine; Democratic senators Mitch Landrieu of Louisiana and Blanche Lincoln of Arkansas; some staunch liberals, such as senators Tom Harkin of Iowa and Carl Levin of Michigan; and some archconservatives, such as senators Tom Coburn of Oklahoma and Jeff Sessions of Alabama (see fig. 5.1). This coalition is noteworthy in an age of party polarization, when obscure elected officials can become celebrities among their party's base by heckling the president during joint sessions in Congress.

The benefits of appealing to the politics of efficiency in the case of asbestos were twofold. First, the promise of improving efficiency by itself has proven to have cross-party appeal. Second, and equally important, the politics of efficiency is flexible enough to accommodate different ideological spins. For Republicans, policy entrepreneurs could build on the agreed-on need for reform by combining the politics of efficiency with long-standing rhetoric about the excesses of the tort system, which should have appealed to their base with criticisms of trial lawyers and attacks on bogus litigation. For Democrats, policy entrepreneurs could build on the expert consensus for reform by combining the politics of efficiency with the promise of a new program for asbestos workers and their families, which should have appealed to organized labor and programmatic liberals. The ability to combine a policy consensus with credit-claiming arguments on both the left and right is a powerful ingredient for building broad legislative coalitions.

This line of reasoning is consistent with Martha Derthick and Paul Quick's (1985, 238) arguments about the "politics of ideas," which they maintain were central to the implementation of deregulation over the objections of industry groups in the 1980s. They contend that deregulation was successful in part because promarket reforms—which are a familiar brand of the politics of efficiency—built on a broad policy consensus that

Table 5.1. Senators Voting to Waive Ensign's Budgetary Point of Order, by State and Party

Name	State	Party	Name	State	Party
Murkowski	AK	Republican	Talent	MO	Republican
Stevens	AK	Republican	Cochran	MS	Republican
Sessions	AL	Republican	Lott	MS	Republican
Shelby	AL	Republican	Baucus	MT	Democratic
Lincoln	AR	Democratic	Burns	MT	Republican
Kyl	AZ	Republican	Burr	NC	Republican
Feinstein	CA	Democratic	Dole	NC	Republican
Allard	CO	Republican	Hagel	NE	Republican
Dodd	CT	Democratic	Domenici	NM	Republican
Lieberman	CT	Democratic	Dewine	OH	Republican
Carper	DE	Democratic	Voinovich	OH	Republican
Martinez	FL	Republican	Coburn	OK	Republican
Chambliss	GA	Republican	Smith	OR	Republican
Isakson	GA	Republican	Santorum	PA	Republican
Harkin	IA	Democratic	Specter	PA	Republican
Grassley	IA	Republican	Chafee	RI	Republican
Craig	ID	Republican	Alexander	TN	Republican
Bayh	IN	Democratic	Frist	TN	Republican
Lugar	IN	Republican	Cornyn	TX	Republican
Brownback	KS	Republican	Hutchison	TX	Republican
Roberts	KS	Republican	Bennett	UT	Republican
McConnell	KY	Republican	Hatch	UT	Republican
Landrieu	LA	Democratic	Allen	VA	Republican
Vitter	LA	Republican	Warner	VA	Republican
Collins	ME	Republican	Leahy	VT	Democratic
Snowe	ME	Republican	Jeffords	VT	Independent
Levin	MI	Democratic	Kohl	WI	Democratic
Stabenow	MI	Democratic	Enzi	WY	Republican
Coleman	MN	Republican	Thomas	WY	Republican
Bond	MO	Republican	—	—	—

Source: Compiled by the author from US Senate data.

Figure 5.1. Ideological Diversity of Senators Voting to Waive Ensign's Budgetary Point of Order

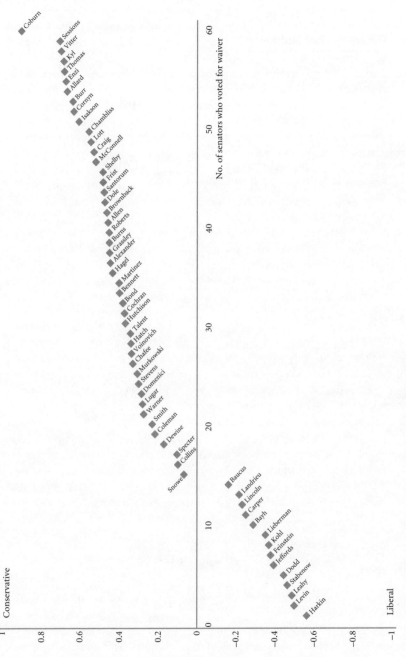

No. of senators who voted for waiver

Source: Compiled by the author from Poole and Rosenthal 2007.

was amenable to both the right and left. Conservatives, led by President Gerald Ford, could tout the benefits of reduced regulation and market competition to business groups and adherents to small government ideology. Likewise, liberals such as Senator Edward Kennedy could extol the virtues of lower prices and the end of government protection of businesses to consumer advocates and organized labor. Derthick and Quirk (1985, 238) conclude: "Within the academic world the convergence was interdisciplinary, and within the political-governmental world it cut across political parties, ideological groupings, and branches of government. Perhaps most important was the convergence of the two worlds when analytic prescriptions, instead of depending upon technical and abstruse arguments, proved adaptable to political rhetoric and position taking."[2] In sum, the politics of efficiency remains an attractive rhetorical gambit, even if it is not a foolproof recipe for legislative success, because it encompasses prescriptions that simultaneously allow members of both parties to take the high policy ground by endorsing expert recommendations while playing partisan politics at the ground level by claiming credit with their core constituencies.

WHAT WENT WRONG WITH THE POLITICS OF EFFICIENCY IN THE CASE OF ASBESTOS?

The politics of efficiency narrowly missed in the case of asbestos litigation reform, which raises questions about its limits as a strategy for building coalitions from the center out. Two lessons stand out, which have particular resonance in the area of civil litigation: (1) The political economy of civil litigation—the ways in which litigation costs and risks structure the interests of individual stakeholders—impedes the politics of efficiency; and (2) the politics of wait and see—the tendency of Congress to defer contentious issues to other branches of government—undermines the politics of efficiency.

The Political Economy of Civil Litigation and the Politics of Efficiency

In general, the politics of efficiency emphasizes collective costs and benefits. The assumption is that the promise of aggregate gains should translate into common political ground among a critical mass of stakeholders. In the case of asbestos, litigation was demonstrably costly and unpredictable, and these general costs and risks had a negative aggregate impact on businesses, organized labor, and claimants in the form of high administrative costs, tightened credit, lower insurance ratings, lost jobs, devalued pensions, and slow and inconsistent payments. Under these circumstances it seems natural for these groups to unite in support of reforms aimed at replacing litigation and eliminating lawyers as intermediaries.

The case of asbestos, however, teaches us that the political economy of civil litigation is not so simple (Epstein 1988). Businesses and insurance companies offer a good case in point. As the major targets of litigation, these groups collectively bear the costs of a successful wave of civil litigation. As such, we might expect them to promote reforms that seek to replace litigation with streamlined administrative alternatives.

Litigation, however, does not spread costs and risks uniformly among potential defendants. Many businesses will not be sued and thus have no stake in reform and may even oppose it on ideological grounds. In addition, not all targets of litigation are equally vulnerable. Some are likely to be better prepared because they are less culpable or have better defenses; some have more insurance; and some are bigger or more profitable. The same is true for insurance companies. Some will not have insured the targets of litigation; some will have spread their risks more effectively through reinsurance markets; and some will have deeper capital reserves. If some businesses and insurers can absorb the costs of lawsuits better than others, they have little reason to favor reforms that benefit their less-resilient (or protected) counterparts (see Leone 1986; Melnick 1998).

In theory, some businesses may even *benefit* from a spate of litigation. Businesses that produce substitute goods and services—such as the producers of alternative insulation materials, in the case of asbestos—might welcome litigation against the producers of rival products because this litigation might drive up the prices of these goods and create opportunities to expand the market share of substitute goods. Even some defendants may indirectly benefit from litigation. The reason is that litigation costs— similar to any form of regulatory costs—serve as a tax that might drive weaker competitors out of their markets while raising barriers to entry for potential competitors. From this perspective, businesses that can manage a sudden influx of lawsuits might secretly applaud the costs of litigation as an anticompetitive boon; indeed, from this vantage, the more inefficient the system, the better.

A parallel set of arguments can be made with respect to victims. From a collective perspective, the costliness and unpredictability of litigation do not serve their overall interests. In practice, however, some victims win the litigation lottery and receive large recoveries, including punitive damages; others do not, even if they have similar claims. This patchwork of winners and losers inevitably means that some claimants will want to preserve the status quo while others will want to change it. These clashing preferences, in turn, create an obstacle to using the politics of efficiency to build broad reform coalitions.

It is important to stress that, although asbestos litigation represents an extreme example in some ways, neither the reliance on torts to address a major public health issue nor the political economy of asbestos litigation is unusual. As Kagan argues in his comparative analysis of the American legal system, "The asbestos story reflects a broader pattern in American governance. Compared to other economically advanced democracies, the United States is distinctive in the relative prominence of private tort actions, rather than social insurance and bureaucratic mechanisms, for seeking compensation for personal injuries and environmentally caused illnesses. The United States is also distinctive in the severity of the legal sanctions (large money damages) available through tort litigation, and in the unpredictability and costliness of its layer-driven, jury-centered methods of adjudication" (Kagan 2001, 127; see also Gifford 2010). This characteristic combination of large verdicts, high costs, and inconsistent payments will yield erratic benefits to claimants and impose variable costs on defendants, which lays the foundation for the type of fractious politics that surrounded the FAIR Act and impeded efforts to overcome the supermajority veto points in the Senate.

The Politics of Wait and See and the Politics of Efficiency

The case of asbestos also illustrates how the politics of wait and see undermines the politics of efficiency. To understand this argument, it is useful to break it into several steps, beginning with its definition and then turning to an explanation of its political relevance to the politics of efficiency and why this dynamic is likely to emerge in other cases.

The politics of wait and see refer to Congress's tendency to defer to other branches of government, which stems from the incentives of the individual members of Congress to avoid contentious issues. Put simply, because the members of Congress face reelection, they have strong incentives to claim credit for vague "feel good" policies while shifting the blame for any tough choices that might alienate potential voters (and campaign contributors) or provide fodder for potential challengers on the campaign

THE ASBESTOS CASE AND THE POLITICS OF EFFICIENCY

trail (see Mayhew 1974; Fiorina 1989; Moe 1989; Arnold 1990; see also Graber 1993; Lovell 2003). Under these circumstances, it is politically tempting to defer the resolution of issues like asbestos injury compensation to the courts, because it avoids making contested trade-offs among the needs of businesses, victims, and professional groups. At a minimum, by staying on the sidelines, the members of Congress can reasonably (and conveniently) wait and see if the courts can settle controversial issues and, if not, learn from the courts' policy mistakes before taking action. Even more cynically, the members of Congress might benefit from problems that linger, because they can claim credit for working on them while asking for campaign contributions and other resources to keep the fight alive.

The problem is that staying on the sidelines is not a politically neutral act. Congressional inertia in the 1980s and 1990s had important ripple effects that continue to radiate through the contemporary politics of asbestos injury compensation. As Congress waited in the 1980s and 1990s, the inefficiency of the asbestos litigation forced overwhelmed private actors and judges to take matters into their own hands and find ways to implement piecemeal court-based tort reforms. Just as new programs create new politics (Campbell 2003; Wilson 1989; Schattschneider 1935), court-based tort reforms create new politics (Barnes 2007a; see also Silverstein 2009).

These new political dynamics reinforced the daunting challenges of passing any replacement reform (Burke 2002) by intensifying the fragmenting effects of the political economy of civil litigation in several ways. First, the implementation of court-based replacement reforms created privately administered trusts that controlled billions of dollars. These trusts gave rise to groups that had significant professional and material stakes in protecting the status quo, such as the Chapter 11 trust professionals. The result was to add another set of reform opponents to an already-crowded field, which included the American Association for Justice's well-organized opposition to the FAIR Act. Second, the Chapter 11 Trusts and various group settlement mechanisms exacerbated the internal splits among business interests. Put simply, some high-exposure defendants have used the tools of court-based replacement reform to manage liability and shift some costs to other businesses in the chain of distribution. In doing so, these trusts have increased the uneven distribution of litigation costs and risks among defendants, adding to the crazy quilt of winners and losers under the existing system and making it even more difficult to find common ground among business interests. From this perspective, for example, advocates for the compensation fund for the victims of September 11, which was enacted in the aftermath of the terrorist attacks, were politically astute to push for the creation of a federal program *before* litigation could ramp up.

It should be added that there is every reason to believe that court-based tort reforms extend beyond the case of asbestos. As a policy matter, asbestos is not the only dangerous product that has caused unexpected losses. Others include coal, DDT, Thalidomide, lead, mercury, tobacco, intrauterine devices, and polyvinyl chlorides. More recent examples include Phen-Fen, an untested or "off-label" combination of federally approved obesity medications linked to increased risk of valvular heart disease, and cox-2 inhibitors, such as Vioxx, Celebrex, and Bextra, a group of medications for arthritis and other inflammation-caused pain, which were linked to increased risks of heart attacks and strokes.

These dangers can create huge classes of claimants, seeking compensation for injuries, lost wages, and diminished quality of life, along with retribution for any corporate wrongdoing that contributed to their losses. Some of these claimants will turn to private insurance, some will rely on preexisting social-benefit programs, and some will lobby Congress and state legislatures for new programs. However, some will inevitably turn to the courts, ensuring that litigation will remain a significant part of the American response to the problem of defective products and other unexpected losses.[3] Indeed, plaintiffs' lawyers in the United States—freed from restrictions on advertising and energized by the prospect of claiming one-third of their clients' recovery though contingency fees, a practice banned in other countries—have built a large and permanent "tort industry" (Kagan 2001, 133). This industry has proven remarkably adept and increasingly sophisticated in inventing new legal causes of action, advertising its services, locating clients, and devising strategies for bringing suits in litigation-friendly jurisdictions.

Whenever there is a sudden surge of litigation, court-based reform will represent an important potential avenue for institutional change. As a legal matter the tools of court-based tort reform—group settlements, Chapter 11 reorganizations, and others—are available in other policy domains. As a practical matter we should expect that various interests will continue to finds ways to use these legal tools creatively. The simplest reason is that judges, who have limited staffs, and plaintiffs' lawyers, who are typically organized into small firms, lack the resources to apply the machinery of litigation to every case. Defense lawyers, meanwhile, have every incentive to adapt the tools of court-based reform to new circumstances in order to limit their clients' exposure to legal obligations, and they have done so, using Chapter 11 to rewrite union contracts, reduce pension obligations, and avoid environmental clean-up costs. Under these circumstances we should see court-based tort reform as a fixture in American politics, which will continue to complicate the use of the politics of efficiency to promote the reforms designed to reduce the chronic costs and uncertainty that inevitably flow from reliance on litigation to make policy.

Before wrapping up the discussion on the politics of efficiency, a somewhat technical caveat about the generalizability of the asbestos case should be addressed for the sake of completeness. It holds that, as a legal matter, the Bankruptcy Amendments of 1994 create a special provision for asbestos-related bankruptcies that does not apply to other policy areas. Specifically, Section 524(g) of the bankruptcy code governs the use of channeling injunctions in asbestos-related reorganizations. These injunctions are crucial to Chapter 11 trusts because they direct all asbestos lawsuits—both pending and future—to the trust and away from the newly reorganized entity. Under Section 524(g) these injunctions may be granted if, among other things, the trust is funded by stock in the reorganized company and at least 75 percent of the trust's beneficiaries have approved the plan of reorganization.

Although Section 524(g) is limited to asbestos cases, the use of Chapter 11 to manage liability is not (Peterson 1990; Vairo 2004). Other companies facing "mass tort" claims have used Chapter 11 to implement court-based replacement reform; these include A. H. Robins, the maker of the intrauterine device the Dalkon Shield; and Dow Corning, the maker of silicone breast implants. There is no reason to think that other companies will not do so in the future. In fact, according to practitioners, defendants in other sectors of the economy may be *more likely* to avail themselves of Chapter 11 than asbestos defendants because Section 524(g) requires such a large amount of the companies' equity to be shifted to claimants.

FINAL THOUGHTS ON THE POLITICS OF EFFICIENCY

In sum, the asbestos case is more than just a typical account of the difficulties of navigating veto points on Capitol Hill in an age of polarized parties and slim majorities. The failure of the FAIR Act provides a useful window into the broader politics of efficiency and allows us to generate some hypotheses about its likely promise and limits. Most interestingly, this case highlights how the combination of inefficient policies and congressional inertia engenders the creation of ad hoc private and judicial exit and cost-shifting strategies by those most adversely affected by existing arrangements. Once these ad hoc strategies are implemented, pressure for systemic reforms is likely to dissipate and the beneficiaries of these strategies are likely to shift from potential reform advocates to probable reform proponents, which complicates the vexing task of building winning institutional reform coalitions. From this vantage, a key obstacle to the politics of efficiency is not always the internecine partisan warfare among polarized parties in Congress—the politics of efficiency has a respectable record of bridging partisan divides—but complex interbranch dynamics that shift the institutional context of congressional action by creating new sources of resistance to reform and thus offer partial exit strategies that reduce the sense of urgency for reform and internally divide groups that might otherwise become reform advocates.

These dynamics and the resulting failure of the politics of efficiency in the case of asbestos raise basic questions about the prospects for and nature of institutional change in an age of slim majorities, polarized parties, and supermajority requirements in the Senate. The last chapter explores this issue, places the patterns of interbranch relations in the asbestos case in context, and considers the implications of these dynamics for those interested in understanding today's policymaking and institutional change in other cases.

NOTES

1. Recall that this total includes Senator Frist, who switched his vote at the last minute to preserve the option to bring a motion to reconsider but had clearly indicated his support of the FAIR Act.

2. Of course, deregulation succeeded and asbestos litigation reform failed. A key difference, however, was probably institutional, not rhetorical. In the case of deregulation, an independent regulatory commission could act in lieu of Congress, thus bypassing the arduous lawmaking process on Capitol Hill (Derthick and Quirk 1985, 243).

3. Patterns of actual claiming practices in the United States are interesting. Research shows that, contrary to public perception, the vast majority of Americans who suffer injuries do not file tort suits. A comprehensive 1988–89 survey, for instance, found that only 10 percent of injured Americans each year even considered filing a claim, only 7 percent contacted an attorney, and only 2 percent filed a lawsuit (Hensler et al. 1991, 122, table 5.2). It also found that the tort system accounts for only 10.5 percent of total economic losses resulting from injuries

THE ASBESTOS CASE AND THE POLITICS OF EFFICIENCY

(ibid, 108, table 4.22). Even in the area of medical malpractice, a perceived hotbed of tort litigation, only one of eight victims makes a claim (see Weiler 1991; Weiler et al. 1993; Danzon 1986, 42; Bell and Connell 1997, 105; Burke 2002, 2–4).

It would be a mistake, however, to underestimate the importance of tort in the United States. First, aggregate data obscure variation in payment sources across settings. Tort plays a more prominent role in some areas, less in others. Thus the same survey that finds tort provides 10.5 percent of compensation for economic losses for all accidents also finds that tort accounts for 31.5 percent of compensation for motor vehicle accidents while providing only 7.5 percent of compensation for work-related accidents (Hensler et al. 1991, 108, table 4.22). And of course tort has played a major role in a number of substantively important cases, including compensation issues arising from the use of tobacco, asbestos, intrauterine devices, and many other products. Second, as a policy matter, tort law represents more than just a source of compensation; it significantly defines potential liability—in terms of both who can be held liable and for how much. On this score, tort often remains conceptually and legally primary in the United States. For example, in most states, juries in tort cases cannot even hear evidence about compensation received from other sources under the "collateral source rule." Why? Tort takes precedence and divulging this information may undermine tort's moral and deterrent aims, which require defendants to pay fully for their actions. The practice sharply differs abroad; in other industrial countries, national social insurance programs have priority over tort in that tort damages are limited to economic losses not already covered and noneconomic damages are legally capped at moderate amounts (Kagan 2001, 131).

CHAPTER 6

The Asbestos Case, Institutional Change, and the Judicialization of American Policymaking

A t first glance, the asbestos case seems to illustrate conventional wisdom about the limited capacity of the American policymaking process for change. Indeed, it seems to be a textbook illustration of how fragmentation and checks and balances thwart change by creating multiple veto points, which make it easier to block reforms than to pass them. After all, the demise of the FAIR Act is only the latest example of failure in this area. Dozens of reform initiatives have died on Capitol Hill since the mid-1970s, whereas asbestos litigation and its related costs and inefficiencies have continued to spiral out of control.

A central lesson of the previous chapters, however, is that viewing the behavior of any single branch of government in isolation can be misleading. In fact, a Congress-based account would tell precisely the wrong story. By viewing the case of asbestos from the perspective of interbranch interactions, one can see that legislative inertia masks a shifting landscape of institutional responses. Put simply, the American system of "separated institutions sharing powers" (Neustadt 1990, 34) not only creates multiple veto points, as is often emphasized, but also offers multiple access points that allow innovation in other forums to flow as legislation ebbs (see Barnes 2008; Melnick 1994). Thus, Congress's inability to act did not provide a decisive blow to reform efforts; rather, it has coexisted and even ironically spurred significant (albeit suboptimal, decentralized, and ad hoc) institutional change in the courts (Barnes 2007a).

This chapter fleshes out this part of the asbestos story in two steps. First, looking back, it describes how change has emerged in the shadow of legislative inertia in the case of asbestos and, equally important, how these subtle modes of change have interacted over time with one another and Congress's failure to act. In so doing, it builds on a growing literature on how modern welfare states evolve (see Mahoney and Thelen 2010; Streeck and Thelen 2005; Hacker 2004; Thelen 2003; Schickler 2001; Clemens and Cook 1999; Weir 1992).[1] And it stresses that partisan battles on Capitol Hill are only the tip of a very large iceberg of activity, which often entails major policy and institutional developments that emerge outside the spotlight of public and media attention.

Second, looking forward, this chapter offers some thoughts about how we should study institutional change and contemporary policymaking. The gist is that we need to move beyond narrow analyses of single branches of government that predominate in the media and academic scholarship and adopt a more holistic perspective on American policymaking that focuses on the interactions among the United States' overlapping and diversely representative policymaking forums (Barnes 2009b; Silverstein 2009; Barnes and Miller 2004a, 2004b). This approach may be labor intensive and less parsimonious than specialized studies, but it offers a more complete and accurate picture of how the US system functions in an age of ideological polarization and narrow partisan majorities in Congress.

LOOKING BACK AT THE ASBESTOS CASE

The asbestos case illustrates at least three characteristic mechanisms of institutional change in the absence of legislation, illustrating what Jacob Hacker (2004, 246–49) calls "drift," the shift in the impact of programs on social life through changing circumstances; "conversion," the reinterpretation of existing rules and programs; and "layering," the adding of new institutional arrangements without eliminating old ones (see Streeck and Thelen 2005). Each is briefly discussed here.

The Asbestos Case and Drift: Workers' Compensation Programs

"Drift" is perhaps the most subtle form of institutional change in social policy. It involves the silent transformation of the effect of institutions and policies on social life due to changing circumstances, as when institutions and policies remain fixed while new risks emerge (Hacker 2004). The failure of workers' compensation programs to adapt to rising asbestos workers' claims in the late 1960s offers a classic illustration of drift.

As discussed in chapter 2, asbestos workers initially turned to state workers' compensation programs, not the courts, as they began to fall ill in growing numbers following World War II. In seeking compensation from these programs, they soon confronted at least two obstacles. First, these programs were designed to compensate workers for traumatic injuries, such as broken limbs, and not slowly manifesting occupational diseases, such as asbestosis and mesothelioma. As a result, asbestos workers' claims often fell outside the programs' preexisting categories of injury and ran afoul of the existing claiming rules, which required them to bring claims within two or three years of their initial injury even though their illnesses often took decades to manifest. Second, employers and insurance companies fought asbestos workers' claims tooth and nail, ensuring that the existing rules were construed narrowly and did not adjust to the influx of new claims. The combination of institutional stability at the state level—workers' compensation programs remained unchanged on the books—and a rising tide of claims that failed to fit preexisting conditions produced drift, which rendered existing programs inadequate and shifted the lion's share of the risks associated with asbestos exposure to workers and their families.

The Asbestos Case and Judicial Conversion: The Rise of Tort Litigation

Drift was only the first round of institutional evolution in the shadow of legislative inertia in the case of asbestos, as workers sought to supplement stingy and uncertain compensation benefits from other sources. Specifically, as early proposals for legislative reforms died in Congress,[2] they increasingly turned to the tort system in the late 1960s and 1970s, seeking to take advantage of new medical findings that connected asbestos exposure to various diseases and an evolving theory of products liability set forth in Section 402A of the second edition of the *Restatement of the Law of Torts*, which held that, if manufacturers fail to warn users of a product's dangers, they are strictly liable for resulting harms, even if the product is unavoidably unsafe.

The scope of this novel theory, however, was far from clear. Defendants strenuously argued that Section 402A was never intended to cover these types of claims. In fact, W. Page Keeton, a preeminent expert on torts and an author of the *Restatement*, testified under oath that Section 402A did not apply to products like asbestos, which had few known substitutes and served beneficial purposes (e.g., fireproofing ships) (Brodeur 1986, 66). Yet the courts interpreted Section 402A broadly in cases like *Borel* (1973), *Karjala* (1975), and *Moran* (1982), and, in the process, stretched—or converted—common-law tort principles to meet the growing (and increasingly urgent) demands of asbestos workers.

As is often the case, judicial conversion did not generate abrupt shifts. It occurred gradually in the 1970s and accelerated in the 1980s, after plaintiffs found the Sumner Simpson papers and other smoking-gun evidence that some manufacturers had knowingly concealed the risks of asbestos. In 1976, 159 cases were reportedly filed against the Johns-Manville Corporation, the leading asbestos mining company and manufacturer in the United States. In 1978, 792 claims were filed against Johns-Manville. In 1982, the year it filed for bankruptcy, the company faced 6,000 new claims per year (Brodeur 1986). Although gradual, the institutional effects were transformational, as the eventual onslaught of litigation added hundreds of thousands of privately funded tort suits to limited workers' compensation program claims.

The Asbestos Case and Judicial Layering: Court-Based Tort Reform

Judicial conversion of tort law did not repair the gaps in the social safety net left by drifting workers' compensation programs. Instead, as we now know, asbestos litigation provided a woefully inefficient and inconsistent means of compensating victims of asbestos-related diseases. These costs produced a chorus of calls for congressional action, but Congress failed to act.

Once again, the combination of ongoing claims, shortcomings of existing institutional arrangements, and congressional inaction created pressure for reform outside the legislative process. This pressure in turn unleashed waves of court-based tort reform, including court-based discouragement, management, and replacement reforms aimed at containing the costs of asbestos litigation. The result was judicial layering, which added new administrative remedies on top of existing tort law and workers' compensation programs (see table 2.4 for a summary of the key institutional differences among workers' compensation programs, tort suits, and Chapter 11 trusts).

Just as judicial conversion failed to offer a policy antidote for administrative drift, piecemeal court-based tort reforms, even court-based replacement reforms, have not wholly ameliorated the costs of asbestos litigation. Instead, as discussed in chapter 2, they have produced mixed results. On the one hand, the Chapter 11 trusts probably have saved some companies significant transaction costs and reduced delays for the processing of some claims. On the other hand, these trusts typically have paid only pennies on the dollar, reflecting the availability of trust funds as opposed to the merits of the underlying claims. Meanwhile, these shortfalls have encouraged further litigation, as lawyers have sought new defendants under the rules of joint and several liability and other theories. As a result, the more individual defendants have used Chapter 11 to manage their liability, the more asbestos tort litigation has spread as entrepreneurial trial lawyers reach ever deeper into the chain of distribution, which, in the case of asbestos, stretches across thousands of businesses regardless of their culpability with respect to fomenting the underlying health crisis.[3]

Judicial Innovation and Congressional Inertia

The failure of court-based tort reform to resolve the asbestos crisis produced pressure for yet another round of reform. By this time, however, judicial innovation seemed exhausted, as the courts themselves urged Congress to act. Unfortunately, the courts' earlier reforms and the resulting judicial layering seemed to undermine congressional action on several fronts. It hindered efforts to pass comprehensive reform in Congress by creating partial exit strategies for some claimants that reduced pressure for a congressional overhaul, introducing new veto players into the process, such as the Chapter 11 trust professionals who have a vested interest in the status quo, and further fracturing the winners and losers on the ground, which has increased divisions among shareholders within and across party lines.

Putting these pieces together reveals an intricate feedback loop connecting legislative inertia, administrative drift, and judicial innovation (see fig. 6.1). In this interaction, the failure of Congress and state legislatures to reform workers' compensation programs to address new risks associated with asbestos-related diseases produced drift, which left asbestos workers and their families inadequately protected. This gap in the social safety net created pressure for action, which led judges to convert general common-law principles to try to meet the needs of asbestos workers and their families. However, the resulting onslaught of litigation predictably engendered a costly and inefficient means of compensation. In the absence of legislative tort reform, courts creatively developed strategies for implementing court-based reforms, which added new layers of institutional responses to the existing ones. These reforms may have reduced some of

Figure 6.1.   Interbranch Patterns of Institutional Change in the Asbestos Case

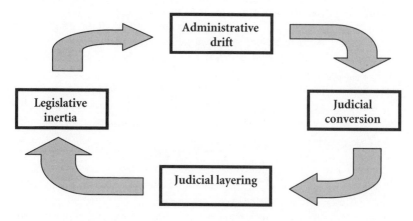

the excesses of litigation for selected individual stakeholders, but they have also helped to undermine efforts at comprehensive legislative reform and thus have helped to reinforce the existing, court-centered response to the asbestos crisis in the United States. As a result, the erratic beat of judicial policymaking goes on, despite the need for more synchronized action (see also Silverstein 2009; Pierson 2004).

Placing This Pattern of Drift and Development in Context

There are reasons to suspect that this pattern of administrative drift and court-based policy development will recur. According to Hacker (2004, 248), drift has been the "most pervasive dynamic" in US social policy since the 1980s. Indeed, in many ways, contemporary American politics seem hardwired for administrative drift, reflecting a combination of dynamic social conditions and stagnant social programs. Thus, as shown in the asbestos case, modern societies generate waves of unforeseen risks for ordinary citizens from market shifts, technological innovations, and hidden dangers and latent defects of widely used products. At the same time, creating new social programs or expanding existing ones through the legislative process is an uphill political battle. As new risks emerge and programs remain unchanged, drift inevitably results.

As cracks in the welfare state appear, some may be willing to shoulder these burdens, but others will inevitably seek protection. As noted in the last chapter, disgruntled interests have several choices of forums when seeking compensation. They can lobby legislatures for new programs or for reforms of existing ones, they can negotiate with their employers for greater benefits, and they might seek private insurance. They can also file lawsuits. Resorting to litigation in at least some cases seems likely if, for no other reason, that entrepreneurial trial lawyers working on contingency fees, like Ward Stephenson, have strong financial incentives to find disaffected interests and frame their grievances in terms of pliable legal rules, such as tort law.

At the same time, members of Congress have several reasons to allow the courts to take the policymaking lead in today's politically charged legislative environment (Farhang 2010; Burke 2002; Kagan 2001, 1994; Barnes 1997). The first is that conflict between Congress and the president, which inevitably arises during periods of divided government, encourages members to rely on litigation as a means of policymaking because it bypasses bureaucracies in the executive branch (Farhang 2010). Burke (2002, 15) calls this the "insulation incentive" and adds that activists also often prefer entrusting implementation to the courts, whose decentralized structure allows them ongoing access to the policymaking process through the assertion of legal claims, which they can control, as opposed to relying on a single federal agency that might be captured by their political rivals, who might lock them out of the process (see also Barnes 1997).

Second, in an era of narrow and shifting majorities, members of the majority party are painfully aware that they may soon become part of the minority and thus lose control over the tools to goad agencies into action. By ensuring enforcement through litigation, members of Congress can manage this political uncertainty by outsourcing enforcement to lawyers, who are free from congressional control and have strong financial incentives to question agencies' decision making (Farhang 2010). Burke adds that this strategy shifts enforcement costs to private litigants, which should be appealing to members on both sides of the aisle because it promises benefits without paying for them (Burke 2002, 16). Finally, privatizing enforcement through litigation avoids contentious battles over program design and thus circumvents the lawmaking obstacle course in Washington (Farhang 2010; see also Moe 1989; Graber 1993; Lovell 2003).

Consistent with these arguments, changes in the structure of the American state since the late 1960s have greatly extended the courts' policymaking reach (Kagan 2001). Beginning in the late 1960s and 1970s, American reformers successfully pushed for new programs that sought to address widespread social problems, such as discrimination, environmental degradation, and consumer safety. To prevent these new agencies from being unduly influenced by the industries they were supposed to regulate, reformers created a series of procedural mechanisms, such as public comment periods and citizen suits, that give the public—and litigation-savvy public interest groups—a voice in administrative decision making and direct means to hold agencies accountable in court. Congress has also found ways to encourage the filing of lawsuits, such as the provision of fee-shifting statutes to ensure that defendants will subsidize the costs of successful litigation against them. The result has been a set of decentralized, rights-based programs that feature high levels of litigation and judicial policymaking (Kagan 1994, 2001; Burke 2002; Melnick 2004; Farhang 2008, 2010; Silverstein 2009).

During the same period, the courts were busily extending their power through expansive readings of common-law doctrines, constitutional law, and administrative rules. The asbestos case offers one example. Another is the landmark Supreme Court decision *Goldberg v. Kelly* (1970), which required hearings for those facing the loss of welfare benefits and touched off a "due process revolution" in regulatory proceedings. This revolution, in turn, led to the creation of a myriad of lawyer-intensive administrative hearings that could be appealed to the courts as well as a constitutional basis for objecting to the fairness of agency decisions (Burke 2001; Melnick 2004). Meanwhile, federal judges relaxed the traditional limitations on bringing private actions against agencies, which further opened the door to litigation by public interest groups (see, generally, Stewart and Sunstein 1982).

The convergence of these changes has had a predictable and profound effect on judicial power in the United States. Today's federal judges not only serve their traditional role of resolving politically important constitutional and common-law disputes (e.g., the asbestos case) but also play a significant role in adjudicating conflicts over the meaning of statutes, deciding public challenges to regulatory procedures, and reviewing agency decisions under the "hard look" doctrine, which can serve as a doctrine of judicial second-guessing (Melnick 2004). As a result, federal judges shape issues that lie far beyond the reach of their counterparts abroad, such as coal mine safety (Braithewaite 1985), nursing home care (Day and Klein 1987), educational opportunity (Kirp 1979), labor relations (Bok 1971), new drugs (Teff 1987), air pollution (Lundqvist 1980), the use of polyvinyl chlorides (Badaracco 1985), and so on (Kagan 2001; see also Kagan and

Axelrad 1994). When placed within these historical trends, the asbestos case is not an anomaly but part of the general rise in "adversarial legalism" in the United States—the use of litigation to make and implement public policy (Kagan 2001; Burke 2002; Melnick 1989, 1994, 2004)—and its patterns of court-based policy development are a small piece in the much larger mosaic of the judicialization of American politics and policymaking (Silverstein 2009; Farhang 2010; see also Schuck 1986; Rabkin 1989; Derthick 2005; Gifford 2010).

LOOKING FORWARD: STUDYING POLICYMAKING IN OTHER CASES

If nothing else, the story of court-based policy development underlying the asbestos case fundamentally challenges the standard descriptions of American policymaking and separation of powers, which assume that the elected branches negotiate fundamental policy decisions; that federal and state agencies implement these legislative bargains according to detailed regulations; and that the courts serve as referees, which resolve disputes, impose legal sanctions for rule violations, and protect basic constitutional rights. Yet in the case of asbestos, the courts, not Congress, have set the basic policy of who pays, how much, and to whom. Moreover, it is the courts, not Congress or agencies, that remain in the vanguard of reforming the basic institutional structures and rules that govern the implementation of asbestos injury compensation policy.

The blurring of the already-fuzzy lines between executive, legislative, and judicial functions in an age of revved-up adversarial legalism and judicialization greatly complicates the task of studying American politics, policymaking, and institutional development. Instead of confronting these puzzles directly, contemporary political scientists have tended to specialize, breaking the process into parts and concentrating on its individual components. The result is armies of narrow congressional, court, presidency, and bureaucracy scholars, who rarely talk to one another. One might reasonably counter that specialization is a tried-and-true response to the problem of complexity, and it has yielded superb research traditions in the fields of American politics, public law, and public administration that continue to bear fruit. But specialization has its price. Substantively, American politics, policymaking, and institutional change are not created on an assembly line. They are deeply interactive. As a result, taking snapshots of the behavior of any single branch of government, however sophisticated the lens, can provide an incomplete and even misleading picture (Barnes 2009a).

As we have seen throughout this case study, a Congress-centric approach would offer an impoverished understanding of both the politics and policy of asbestos injury compensation. Without an understanding of how litigation has shifted the political economy of asbestos litigation reform, the interest group politics of the FAIR Act would remain a mystery, a seeming example of "false consciousness," as some stakeholders seemed to work tirelessly against reforms aimed at advancing their collective interests. Yet once we appreciate how litigation imposes uneven costs and risks among stakeholders, the internal divisions among the resulting winners and losers make perfect sense. Similarly, as discussed in this chapter, the failure to account for how congressional inertia interacted with existing administrative programs and encouraged judicial innovation would miss the dynamic landscape of institutional change that underlies decades of failed legislation.

This is not simply a reminder that American policymaking is messy and that simplified models are likely to miss things. It is a call to align the study of politics, policymaking, and institutional change with viable conceptions of the American state (Barnes 2008; see also Orren and Skowronek 2004). In nations with well-defined divisions of labor among various governmental actors, stable institutional arrangements, and limited access points, a narrow focus on individual parts of the process may be sensible. However, the United States does not feature well-defined and stable institutional arrangements that govern discrete policy areas, even on relatively narrow issues. Instead, the modern American administrative state rests on constellations of overlapping and interacting policymaking forums that feature distinct historical legacies, norms of reasoning, structural barriers, and constituencies. If we want to make sense of policymaking and institutional change within this kind of state, we must attend to recurring patterns across the various branches and levels of government over time (Barnes and Miller 2004a, 2004b; Barnes 2007a; Silverstein 2009).

Of course, an interbranch approach is labor intensive and is likely to produce less parsimonious and generalizable accounts of American politics. However, the benefits are a better conceptual understanding of the process, especially the political relevance of seemingly technical legal matters (Barnes 2007a, 2009b; see also Feeley and Rubin 1998; Shapiro 1964, 1968, 1981). Indeed, once one adopts an interbranch perspective, the political significance of even arcane aspects of the litigation process suddenly come into focus and open new vistas of inquiry for scholars of public law as well as American politics and public administration. For example, an interbranch perspective teaches us that the Federal Rules of Civil Procedure are not only legal rules that guide the filing and conduct of federal litigation but are also a framework that governs a distinct mode of policymaking that has played a central role in a myriad of important political issues, including the various struggles for equality, the fight against environmental degradation, and efforts to improve consumer safety (Barnes 2009b). Within this framework of judicial policymaking, contingency fees not only fund litigation but also support an energetic class of policy entrepreneurs who mobilize individuals who might not otherwise act. Discovery is not only a method for uncovering evidence for trial but is also a means of information gathering during the policymaking process. Chapter 11 reorganizations are not only a procedure to rationalize the claim process against financially distressed companies but are also a tool for businesses to retrench private rights of action on an ad hoc basis. And the battle over tort reform is not only a political fight over access to the courts but is also part of a larger struggle over the reach of social benefits in the public–private welfare state in the United States. These types of redescriptions, in turn, challenge those interested in American politics and policymaking to adopt a more integrated interbranch approach, which rightfully brings the law, the courts, and litigation back into their analyses (Barnes 2007a, 2008; Barnes and Miller 2004a, 2004b; Silverstein 2009).

NOTES

1. The definition of "institutions" and thus institutional change is enormously complex (Scott 2008). This book makes no attempt to describe these debates, much less resolve them. Instead, it follows leading studies of contemporary welfare states and treats institutions as rules that may be enforced by a third party (e.g., Streeck and Thelen 2005, 10). For the purposes of this analysis, which focuses on asbestos injury compensation, institutional change means significant shifts in the rules governing who decides, who pays, how much, and to whom.

2. The first congressional efforts to overhaul asbestos litigation appeared in the early 1970s. Specifically, on April 12, 1973, before the Court of Appeals for the Fifth Circuit handed down *Borel*, Republican representative Frelinghuysen introduced the first federal replacement reform bill titled the Asbestosis and Mesothelioma Benefits Act (HR 6906). The bill was targeted. It sought to provide benefits to asbestos workers suffering from asbestosis and mesothelioma, who often fell through the cracks of workers' compensation programs. The bill was cosponsored by members on both sides of the aisle, whose Americans for Democratic Action scores ranged from very conservative (6.64 out of 100) to moderate (49.67 out of 100) to very liberal (92.69 out of 100). Despite its narrow focus and bipartisan

sponsorship, the bill died in the House Committee on Education and Labor without a hearing. (Other asbestos injury compensation bills met a similar fate throughout the 1970s and early 1980s.)

3. Of course, as a legal matter, these companies might have a cause of action against other, more culpable firms. However, as a practical matter, most of the original defendants are now defunct, leaving in their wake a series of undercapitalized trusts.

The Case Method and "Likely" Cases

Case studies present a conundrum for social scientists. As John Gerring (2007, 8) powerfully argues, "Although much of what we know about the empirical world has been generated by case studies, and case studies continue to constitute a large proportion of the work generated by the social science disciplines, . . . the case study *method* is generally unappreciated—arguably, because it is poorly understood" (emphasis in the original). The underappreciation, and, in some cases, outright hostility toward case studies is particularly paradoxical given growing concerns about the application of standard regression analysis to nonexperimental data drawn from complex social and political settings. These critiques, which are by now familiar to social scientists, include the difficulty of specifying adequate models given the number of potentially relevant variables and their possible interactions, the arbitrariness of standard significance tests, the omnipresent problem of measurement error, the misleading precision of point estimates in curve fitting models, the difficulty of assessing causal mechanisms from correlations, and so on (see, generally, Achen 1986; Chatfield 1995; Kittel and Winner 2005; Winship and Sobel 2005; Gerring 2007).

Part of the problem is the fog of false dichotomies that plagues discussions of social science methodologies and obscures the place of case studies in the ongoing practice of social science along with their underlying strengths and weaknesses. For example, some scholars associate case studies with qualitative as opposed to quantitative methods, drawing a sharp distinction between studies that tell stories and studies that count. However, as seen in the preceding pages, case studies do not preclude the use of quantitative methods. Indeed, the norm is to include both quantitative and qualitative analyses within case studies and to use diverse analytic tools to triangulate the empirical findings that are woven into the final narrative.

Another common but potentially misleading distinction is between "variable-oriented" research, which looks at a discrete number of factors across many cases, and "case-oriented" research, which explores configurations of factors within a single or small set of cases. These analytic approaches are surely different, given that they encompass fundamentally distinct assumptions about the nature of complex social phenomena and causation (Ragin 2000). But these approaches are complements, not rivals, because different areas of inquiry may be more or less compatible with variable-based or case-oriented assumptions (Gerring 2007, 12–13). Moreover, all case studies—implicitly or explicitly—are selected from populations of cases and thus are embedded in an analysis of several key variables or likely clusters of factors across cases. The better we are able to locate a single case in a population of cases along several theoretically relevant dimensions—whether these dimensions are conceptualized as arrays of discrete variables or interconnected configurations of them—the better we can assess what we are studying and what are its potential contributions and limits.

Finally, some lump case studies under the (often-pejorative) label of "small-N" research, as contrasted with (often-preferred) "large-N" studies that rely on surveys or broad data sets that collect many observations across multiple cases. Yet one of the *advantages* of case studies is that researchers can go "back to the case" and generate new data that probe the observable implications of alternative explanations as well as consider ways to divide their cases cross-sectionally and temporally to generate new frames of comparisons and thus "stretch" the available N. As a result case studies often rest on an enormous number of observations from diverse sources, albeit within the confines of a limited set of contexts. It is often the convergence of findings based on multiple observations from diverse sources, each with their own distinctive sets of limitations and biases, that lends case studies their internal validity.

It is best then to understand case studies as providing one set of tools for building insight into existing theories about the complex world that surrounds us (see, generally, Lijphart 1971; Eckstein 1975; Skocpol and Somers 1980; Collier 1993; George and Bennett 2005; Gerring 2004, 2007). Like any tool, case studies are better suited for some jobs than others and should not lie alone in a researcher's tool kit. Moreover, just as there are different kinds of screwdrivers, there are many kinds of case studies, each with its place in the research cycle in which theories are generated, tested, reformulated, and tested again.

This book has framed the story of asbestos litigation reform as a "likely" case study. Likely case studies are selected from a population of cases because recognized explanatory factors (or "independent variables") within the literature point toward an outcome—but this outcome does not occur (George and Bennett 2005). The promise of a likely case design is ultimately a function of the nature of the underlying theory in question. If the underlying theory posits that a factor is a necessary condition for an outcome or that a factor, if present, is sufficient to cause an outcome, then a most likely case can serve to disprove theory and, through careful tracing of processes, generate new hypotheses about the outcome to be explained (the "dependent variable") (see Bennett 2010).

Many social science theories—and certainly the theories about the prospects of passing major civil litigation reforms in the United States—are probabilistic, not deterministic. No one argues that Republican majorities *guarantee* the passage of major tort reform or that Congress *always* acts when the Supreme Court urges legislative action. Instead these factors should increase the likelihood of congressional action. In this theoretical environment a likely case cannot be used to disprove existing theories because any single case may represent nothing more than an anomaly. Equally important, probabilistic theories *assume* that the relationship among factors varies, so that the absence of a relationship in a single case is not necessarily inconsistent with the theory's predictions. In short, in a world of probabilistic theories, likely cases are not well suited for hypothesis *testing*.

Hypothesis *generation* is another matter. By tracing processes of failure in cases where we expect success, a historical analysis of a single case can reveal dynamics and factors that have been missed by existing theory. At the same time, it is not enough for the analysis to turn up idiosyncratic factors in relation to a body of probabilistic theory. Such factors may be of intense significance for understanding the case at hand and, as such, their discovery may represent a meaningful *empirical* contribution. But such factors are not necessarily theoretically useful. To be theoretically valuable, the research must show something more. One possibility is to show that the newly identified factors are likely to recur in other cases within the population and may have a plausible probabilistic effect on the dependent variable. In the language of quantitative analysis, these findings must plausibly point to "missing variables," whose omission threatens to bias existing models. Alternatively, the researcher might show how the findings require us to reconceptualize existing variables or shed light on the relationship among variables, such as the direction of causality (Gerring 2007; George and Bennett 2005; Bennett 2010).

Accordingly, the reason that this book focuses on factors like court-based tort reform is not because this factor was necessarily determinative of the demise of the FAIR Act, or even the most important factor relative to others, but because this factor (1) plausibly contributed to its failure, (2) it is likely to emerge in other cases, (3) the failure to account for it in other cases may bias our understanding of the broader phenomenon of tort reform because focusing only on legislation may systematically underestimate the amount and opportunity for institutional change in the United States, and (4) its omission may cause us to overlook how litigation acts as a mechanism for creating crosscutting preferences among stakeholders who might otherwise favor reform. In a field that remains largely undertheorized and is not amenable to the creation of experiments with a truly random assignment of treatments, these types of contributions seem worthwhile because, without a well-developed body of theory, we cannot adequately specify a model that can make nonbiased estimates using the various methods of regression analysis. In short, the value of this research—like any social science research—depends on the state of what is already known. In a field where we are still mapping the basic contours of an intricate causal landscape, zooming in on a single, substantively important case with an eye toward the boundaries of existing theories and concepts can contribute to the store of useful knowledge, even from a somewhat narrow positivist perspective that stresses the importance of hypothesis generation and testing.

Chronology of Selected Events

108TH CONGRESS

November 2002

Republicans pick up seats in Congress during a midterm election—Senate: 51 Republicans, 48 Democrats, 1 Independent; House: 229 Republicans, 205 Democrats, 1 Independent.

Senator Orrin Hatch (R-UT) is named chair of the Senate Judiciary Committee.

February 2003

Senate Budget Committee chair Don Nickles (R-OK) introduces the Claims Criteria and Compensation Act of 2003 (S 413), a medical criteria bill that would leave asbestos claims in the courts but require claims to meet medical standards.

S 413 is referred to the Senate Judiciary Committee.

June 2003

Senator Hatch holds hearings and mark-up sessions on the Fairness in Asbestos Injury Resolution Act (S 1125), or FAIR Act, which would replace litigation with a no-fault trust fund.

July 2003

Senator Hatch agrees to a series of Democratic-sponsored amendments to S 1125 that increase payments and funding of the bill to potentially $153 billion.

Senate Judicial Committee votes 10–8 to approve S 1125, with Senator Dianne Feinstein (D-CA) as the sole Democratic to vote in favor (July 10).

Insurance companies announce that they will fight S 1125.

October 2003

Senate majority leader Bill Frist (R-TN) completes negotiation of a scaled-back trust fund bill; contributions would reportedly be capped at $115 billion.

Congressional Budget Office (CBO) sends a letter to Senator Frist estimating that the fund would need $136 billion to pay claims.

March 2004

CBO sends a revised analysis of the trust fund bill to Senator Hatch saying that the fund would need $123 billion to pay claims (March 24).

April 2004

CBO sends a letter to Senator Nickles and others warning that estimating final claims against the trust fund is uncertain (April 8).

Senator Frist dubs the creation of an asbestos injury compensation trust fund a "personal priority" and introduces his version of the FAIR Act (S 2290), which would create a $124 billion trust fund.

Senate suspends debate on S 2290 after rejecting a motion to invoke cloture (50–47) (April 22).

Senator Frist and Senator Tom Daschle (D-SD), the minority leader, announce that they will ask Judge Edward Becker to mediate among the trust fund bill's stakeholders beginning April 26.

May 2004

Judge Becker decides to end talks on the trust fund bill.

June 2004

Senator Daschle proposes a $141 billion trust fund.

November 2004

President George W. Bush is reelected on a platform calling for asbestos litigation reform.

Republicans increase majorities in the Congress—Senate: 55 Republicans, 44 Democrats, 1 Independent; House: 231 Republicans, 202 Democrats, 1 Independent, 1 vacancy.

Conservatives urge the Senate leadership to bypass Arlen Specter as chair of the Judiciary Committee, in part because of fears that he would block efforts to enact liability reform.

December 2004

Incoming Senate Judiciary Committee chair Specter announces that he will introduce major asbestos litigation reform in the first week of the 109th Congress.

109TH CONGRESS

January 2005

Newly appointed Senate Committee chair Specter begins extensive hearings and negotiation on the creation of an asbestos injury compensation trust fund.

April 2005

Representative Chris Cannon (R-UT) introduces HR 1957, a medical criteria bill that would leave asbestos claims in the courts but require claims to meet medical standards.

May 2005

After months of hearings and negotiations, the Senate Judiciary Committee approves the latest version of the FAIR Act (S 852), which proposes replacing asbestos litigation with a $140 billion trust fund, by a 13–5 vote.

Three Democrats—senators Patrick Leahy (D-VT), Feinstein, and Herb Kohl (D-WI), vote to approve S 852.

At least three conservative senators who voted S 852 out of committee— Tom Coburn (R-OK), John Cornyn (R-TX), and Jon Kyl (R-AZ)— signal that significant changes would have to be made for them to vote for S 852 on the floor.

August 2005

CBO releases report on S 852, finding that the fund would collect a maximum of $140 billion and would receive claims of $120 billion to $150 billion.

September 2005

Bates White, a private consulting firm, releases an analysis that suggests that the proposed trust fund would quickly be overwhelmed by claims.
Senator Specter conducts further hearings on the estimated costs of S 852, receiving contradictory testimony.

November 2005

Government Accountability Office releases a critical report on federal trust funds.
Senator Specter holds additional hearings on future asbestos claims.

February 2006

Senate floor action begins on S 852.
Senator John Ensign (R-NV) brings a budgetary point of order against S 852 based on a prohibition against legislation that would authorize more than $5 billion in spending during any ten-year period starting in 2016.
Motion to waive the point of order—which requires 60 votes—fails in a 58–41 vote.
Senate Majority Leader Frist changes his vote so that he can raise a motion to reconsider and promises to bring S 852 back to the floor if its proponents can muster the missing vote.

May 2006

Senators Specter and Leahy introduce a new bill, S 3274, which makes slight changes to S 852.

November 2006

Republicans lose their majorities in both chambers of Congress—Senate: 50 Democrats, 49 Republicans, 1 Independent (counting Senator Joseph Lieberman [CN], an independent Democrat, as part of the majority); House: 233 Democrats, 202 Republicans.

Classroom Discussion Questions

BACKGROUND QUESTIONS

1. What is meant by "the politics of efficiency"? Why is it relevant to the asbestos case? Do you expect it to be relevant to other policymaking debates? Why?

2. What is the "asbestos crisis"?

3. Why did asbestos workers like Clarence Borel turn to the courts for compensation in the late 1960s and early 1970s?

4. What have been the strengths and weaknesses of litigation as means to compensate victims of asbestos-related diseases?

5. What is "court-based tort reform"? Why did the courts implement these reforms? What were some of the policy and political consequences of these reforms?

THE POLITICS OF THE FAIR ACT

1. Why did the passage of asbestos litigation reform seem likely following the 2004 elections?

2. Why did it fail?

3. Why did asbestos victims divide over the FAIR Act, which promised to replace a system of compensation that was inefficient, unfair, and sometimes fraudulent?

4. Why did business groups divide over the FAIR Act?

5. What was the role of trial lawyers in defeating the FAIR Act?

6. In the end, who benefited from the failure of the FAIR Act? Who lost?

APPENDIX C

LESSONS OF THE CASE STUDY

1. What does Congress's failure to pass the FAIR Act teach us about the promise and limits of the politics of efficiency as a coalition-building strategy?

2. If you were a senator who supported major asbestos litigation reform, what would you have done differently in this case?

3. If you were a judge, what would you have done? Would you have recognized the claims of Clarence Borel and other asbestos victims under the doctrine of strict product liability? Would you have implemented court-based tort reforms, even if you knew that these reforms might undermine congressional efforts to pass comprehensive reforms?

4. What does this case teach us about the current role of courts in the development of public policy in the United States?

5. What does this case imply about the fragmented US policymaking system's capacity for change in an age of narrow majorities and polarized parties in Congress?

6. How does this case change the way you think about the policymaking process in America? Does it make you feel better or worse about it? Why?

7. What is the role of case studies in advancing our theoretical understanding of contemporary American politics?

GLOSSARY OF KEY LEGAL TERMS

"Appellate" versus "trial" courts. Court systems in the United States typically consist of three levels: trial courts that initially hear and decide cases after reviewing evidence, including the examination and cross-examination of witnesses; at least one intermediate appellate court that reviews trial courts' decisions; and a supreme court that reviews intermediate appellate court decisions (see also "US district courts," "US courts of appeal," and "US Supreme Court").

Chapter 11 reorganization. The US bankruptcy code is divided into chapters. Chapter 11 of the bankruptcy code governs reorganizations: a legal process for an entity—typically a partnership or corporation, but sometimes an individual—to negotiate a court-approved plan to keep its business alive, pay its creditors over time, and gain a fresh start.

Chapter 11 trusts. In the context of asbestos litigation, Chapter 11 trusts refer to private compensation schemes for the victims of asbestos-related illnesses that are created as part of Chapter 11 reorganizations. Although the specific terms of Chapter 11 trusts vary, they are typically funded by cash and stock in the newly reorganized company. Trust payments are generally calculated on the basis of detailed medical criteria and benefit schedules. Disbursements from these trusts, which are often insolvent, usually depend on the availability of trust assets.

Class action lawsuits. Class action lawsuits are a form of litigation in which a large group of claims raising common legal and factual issues are aggregated under the names of one or several representatives.

Compensatory damages. Compensatory damages are court-awarded compensation to the plaintiff for actual, out-of-pocket losses caused by the defendant's conduct.

Complaint. A complaint is the document that formally commences a lawsuit. Among other things, the complaint sets forth the plaintiff's basic factual allegations, the underlying legal theories for recovery ("causes of action"), and the compensation sought ("damages"), along with why the court is authorized to decide the case ("subject matter jurisdiction").

Contingency fees. Contingency fees refer to compensation arrangements between lawyers and their clients whereby lawyers agree to accept a percentage of any eventual recovery as opposed to an hourly fee.

GLOSSARY OF KEY LEGAL TERMS

Defendant. A defendant is the target of litigation, that is, the entity that is being sued by the plaintiff.

Discouragement reforms. Discouragement reforms are measures that seek to deter litigation by making lawsuits harder to bring or potentially less lucrative without changing the underlying litigation process. Discouragement reform includes legislation designed to limit (or cap) the amount of damages that can be awarded or judicial interpretations of existing law that limit its scope.

Discovery. Discovery is information gathering during a lawsuit in preparation for trial. Discovery typically includes written questions (interrogatories) and interviews of potential witnesses (depositions), whose statements are transcribed and made under oath. Discovery also usually entails the sharing of documents pursuant to court orders (known as subpoenas *ducas tecum*).

Diversity jurisdiction. To decide a case, courts must have authority or "jurisdiction" over its subject matter. Diversity jurisdiction is a source of federal court subject matter jurisdiction. It generally applies to lawsuits based on state law that involve citizens from different states (or non–US citizens) where the controversy exceeds a minimum amount. In diversity jurisdiction cases, federal courts apply relevant state law.

Docket. A docket is a formal list of cases and proceedings before a court.

FAIR Act. The Fairness in Asbestos Injury Compensation Act, or FAIR Act (S 825), was a classic replacement reform (see below), which proposed supplanting the court-based system of asbestos injury compensation with a $140 billion federal trust fund that would have compensated claimants according to specific medical criteria and would have capped attorneys' fees at 5 percent.

Forum shopping. In the American legal system more than one court or district can have the authority to hear a case. Under these circumstances plaintiffs have a choice of venue. Forum shopping is the strategic filing of a lawsuit in a court or district that is known to be sympathetic to the plaintiff's type of claim.

Inactive dockets. In the context of asbestos litigation, inactive dockets (also known as pleural registries, unimpaired-asbestos dockets, and deferred dockets) refer to the practice of creating a two-tiered system for asbestos lawsuits. Suits by plaintiffs meeting specific medical criteria are allowed to proceed, whereas those by plaintiffs who have been exposed to asbestos but do not (yet) meet these criteria must wait.

Management reforms. Management reforms are measures that seek to streamline the litigation process by simplifying procedures or clarifying substantive rules. Management reforms include legislation that requires alternative dispute resolution or seeks to standardize legal rules (like the American Law Institute's second edition of its *Restatement of the Law of Torts*) or judicial orders that consolidate or standardize the discovery process (see, e.g., multidistrict litigation).

Multidistrict litigation. Multidistrict litigation refers to a federal legal procedure designed to consolidate the discovery and pretrial portions of cases pending in different US court districts that involve one or more common questions of fact.

A specialized judicial panel, the Judicial Panel on Multidistrict Litigation, decides whether cases qualify for multidistrict litigation and where to transfer the cases.

Plaintiff. A plaintiff is the entity that brings a lawsuit against the defendant.

Punitive damages. Punitive damages are court-awarded compensation to plaintiffs beyond their out-of-pocket costs that are intended to punish defendants for egregious conduct and deter similar conduct in the future.

Replacement reforms. Replacement reforms are measures that seek to provide alternatives to the litigation process. Examples include legislation that creates no-fault insurance programs or judicial approval of Chapter 11 trusts (see above).

Section 402A. In the case of asbestos, Section 402A refers to the portion of the American Law Institute's second edition of its *Restatement of the Law of Torts* that recognizes a theory of recovery (or "cause of action") called strict product liability. Under Section 402A, if manufacturers fail to warn users of a product's dangers, they are liable for the resulting harm, even if the product is unavoidably unsafe. Section 402A was adopted by a number of states, including Texas, where Clarence Borel worked as a pipe insulator.

Settlement. In the context of litigation, a settlement refers to a negotiated resolution of a lawsuit.

Tort law. Tort law is a branch of civil law that addresses a plaintiff's right to compensation for personal, property, or reputational harm (not arising from the violation of contracts, which is governed by a separate branch of law, known as contract law) (see, e.g., Section 402A).

US courts of appeal. The ninety-four federal court districts are organized into twelve regional circuits, each of which has a US court of appeals, which hears appeals from the district courts located within its circuit and appeals from decisions of federal administrative agencies.

US district courts. Each state has one or more federal court districts, each of which features a district court. US district courts generally serve as the trial courts in the federal court system.

US Supreme Court. The US Supreme Court is the highest court in the federal court system. It consists of a chief justice and eight associate justices. At its discretion, and within guidelines established by Congress, the Supreme Court hears a limited number of cases from state supreme courts and the US courts of appeal that involve important questions of constitutional or federal law.

REFERENCES

BOOKS AND ARTICLES

Abelson, Alan. 2002. All the Rage. *Barron's*, January 28.

Achen, Christopher H. 1986. *The Statistical Analysis of Quasi-Experiments*. Berkeley: University of California Press.

Aldrich, John. 1995. *Why Parties? The Origin and Transformation on Party Politics in America*. Chicago: University of Chicago Press.

Arnold, Douglass. 1990. *The Logic of Congressional Action*. New Haven, CT: Yale University Press.

Associated Press. 2009. Joe Wilson Becomes GOP Fundraising Star. September 25. www.myfoxdc.com/dpp/new/092509.

Ausness, Richard C. 1994. Tort Liability for Asbestos Removal. *Oregon Law Review* 73:505–50.

Austern, David. 2001. *Memorandum to Manville Trust Claimants*. Fairfax, VA: Claims Management Trust.

Badaracco, Joseph L. 1985. *Loading the Dice: A Five-Country Study of Vinyl Chloride Regulation*. Boston: Harvard Business School Press.

Banaiie, A., B. Auvert, M. Goldberg, A. Guegeuen, and S. Goldberg. 2000. Future Trends in Mortality of French Men from Mesothelioma. *Occupational and Environmental Medicine* 57, no. 7:488–94.

Barnes, Jeb. 1997. Bankrupt Bargain? Bankruptcy Reform and the Politics of Adversarial Legalism. *Journal of Law and Politics* 13, no. 4:893–934.

———. 2007a. Bringing the Courts Back In: Inter-branch Perspectives on the Role of Courts in American Politics and Policy-Making. *Annual Review of Political Science* 10:25–44.

———. 2007b. Rethinking the Landscape of Tort Reform: Lessons from the Asbestos Case. *Justice Systems Journal* 28, no. 2:157–81.

———. 2008. Courts and the Puzzle of Institutional Stability and Change: Administrative Drift and Judicial Innovation in the Case of Asbestos. *Political Research Quarterly* 61:636–48.

———. 2009a. In Defense of Asbestos Litigation: Rethinking Legal Process Analysis in a World of Uncertainty, Second Bests, and Shared Policy-Making Responsibility. *Law & Social Inquiry* 34, no. 1:5–29.

————. 2009b. US District Courts, Litigation, and the Policy-Making Process. In *Exploring Judicial Politics*, edited by Mark Miller. New York: Oxford University Press.

Barnes, Jeb, and Mark Miller. 2004a. Governance as Dialogue. In *Making Policy, Making Law: An Interbranch Perspective*, edited by Mark Miller and Jeb Barnes. Washington, DC: Georgetown University Press.

————. 2004b. Putting the Pieces Together: American Lawmaking from an Interbranch Perspective. In *Making Policy, Making Law: An Interbranch Perspective*, edited by Mark Miller and Jeb Barnes. Washington, DC: Georgetown University Press.

Behrens, Mark A., and Manuel Lopez. 2005. Unimpaired Dockets: Are They Constitutional? *Review of Litigation* 24:253–99.

Bell, Peter, and Jeffrey O'Connell. 1997. *Accidental Justice: The Dilemmas of Tort Law*. New Haven, CT: Yale University Press.

Bennett, Andrew. 2010. Process Tracing and Causal Inference. In *Rethinking Social Inquiry: Diverse Tools, Shared Standards*, edited by Henry E. Brady and David Collier. Lanham, MD: Rowman & Littlefield.

Beth, Richard S., Valerie Heitshusen, and Batsy Palmer. 2010. Filibusters and Cloture in the Senate. Report for Congress RL 30360, Congressional Research Service, March 12.

Bhagavatula, Raji, Rebecca Moody, and Jason Russ. 2001. Asbestos: A Moving Target. *Best's Review*, September 1, 85–90.

Binder, Sarah A. 1998. The Dynamics of Legislative Gridlock, 1947–1996. *American Political Science Review* 93, no. 3:519–33.

Bogus, Carl T. 2001. *Why Lawsuits Are Good for America: Disciplined Democracy, Big Business, and the Common Law*. New York: New York University Press.

Bok, Derek. 1971. Reflections on the Distinctive Character of American Labor Laws. *Harvard Law Review* 84:1461.

Bowker, Michael. 2003. *Fatal Deception: The Untold Story of Asbestos: Why It Is Still Legal and Still Killing Us*. New York: Rodale.

Braithwaite, John. 1985. *To Punish or Persuade: Enforcement of Coal Mine Safety*. Albany: State University of New York Press.

Brodeur, Paul. 1986. *Outrageous Misconduct: The Asbestos Industry on Trial*. New York: Pantheon Books.

Bureau of National Affairs. 1987. *Asbestos Abatement: Risks and Responsibilities*. Washington, DC: BNA, Inc.

Burke, Thomas F. 2001. The Rights Revolution Continues: Why New Rights Are Born (and Old Rights Rarely Die). *Connecticut Law Review* 33:1259–74.

————. 2002. *Lawyers, Lawsuits, and Legal Rights*. Berkeley: University of California Press.

Campbell, Andrea L. 2003. *How Politics Makes Citizens: Senior Political Activism and the American Welfare State*. Princeton, NJ: Princeton University Press.

Campbell, Thomas J., Daniel P. Kessler, and George B. Shepherd. 1995. *The Causes and Effects of Liability Reform: Some Empirical Evidence*. NBER Working Paper 4989. Cambridge, MA: National Bureau of Economic Research.

Cardozo Symposium. 1992. Colloquy: An Administrative Alternative to Tort Litigation to Resolve Asbestos Claims. *Cardozo Law Review* 13 (Collection of Papers Delivered at the Administrative Conference on the United States, October 31, 1991).

Carrington, Paul D. 2007. Asbestos Lessons: The Consequences of Asbestos Litigation. *Review of Litigation* 26:583–612.

Carroll, Stephen J., and Nicholas Pace. 1987. *Assessing the Effects of Tort Reform*. Santa Monica, CA: RAND Institute for Civil Justice.

Carroll, Stephen J., Deborah Hensler, Allan Abrahamse, Jennifer Gross, Michelle White, Scott Ashwood, and Elizabeth Sloss. 2002. *Asbestos Litigation Costs and Compensation: An Interim Report*. Santa Monica, CA: RAND Institute for Civil Justice.

Carroll, Stephen J., Deborah Hensler, Jennifer Gross, Elizabeth M. Sloss, Allan Abrahamse, and J. Scott Ashwood. 2005. *Asbestos Litigation*. Santa Monica, CA: RAND Institute for Civil Justice.

Castleman, Barry. 1996. *Asbestos: Medical and Legal Aspects*, 4th ed. Englewood Cliffs, NJ: Aspen Law & Business.

———. 2005. *Asbestos: Medical and Legal Aspects*, 5th ed. New York: Aspen Publishers.

Cauchon, Dennis. 1999. The Asbestos Epidemic: An Emerging Catastrophe. *USA Today*, February 8.

Chatfield, Chris. 1995. Model Uncertainty, Data Mining and Statistical Inference. *Journal of Royal Statistical Society, Series A (Statistics in Society)* 158, no. 3:419–66.

Clemens, Elisabeth S., and James M. Cook. 1999. Politics and Institutionalism: Explaining Durability and Change. *Annual Review of Sociology* 25:441–66.

Cochran, John. 2004. Religious Right Lays Claims to Big Role in GOP Agenda. *CQ Weekly*, November 13, 2684.

Coffee, John C., Jr. 1995. Class Wars: The Dilemma of the Mass Tort Class Action. *Columbia Law Review* 95:1343–1465.

Collier, David. 1993. The Comparative Method. In *Political Science: State of the Discipline II*, edited by A. Finiter. Washington, DC: American Political Science Association.

Connaught, James L. 1989. Recovery of Risk Comes of Age: Asbestos in Schools and the Duty to Abate a Latent Environmental Hazard. *Northwestern Law Review* 83:512–45.

Connolly, Ceci, and Michael D. Shear. 2009. Obama Implores Congress to Act. *Washington Post*, September 10.

Danzon, Patricia. 1986. *New Evidence on the Frequency and Severity of Medical Malpractice Claim*. Santa Monica, CA: RAND Institute for Civil Justice.

REFERENCES

Day, Patricia, and Rudolf Klein. 1987. The Regulation of Nursing of Homes: A Comparative Perspective. *Milbank Quarterly* 65:303–34.

Derickson, Alan. 1998. *Black Lung: An Anatomy of a Public Health Disaster*. Ithaca, NY: Cornell University Press.

Derthick, Martha. 2005. *Up in Smoke: From Legislation to Litigation in Tobacco Politics*, 2nd ed. Washington, DC: CQ Press.

Derthick, Martha, and Paul J. Quirk. 1985. *The Politics of Deregulation*. Washington, DC: Brookings Institution Press.

Eckstein, Harry. 1975. Case Study and Theory in Political Science. In *Handbook of Political Science*, vol. 7, edited by Fred I. Greenstein and Nelson Polsby. Reading, MA: Addison-Wesley.

Eisenberg, Theodore, and James A. Henderson Jr. 1992. Inside the Quiet Revolution in Products Liability. *UCLA Law Review* 39:731–810.

Elliott, Euel, and Susette Talarico. 1991. An Analysis of Statutory Development: The Correlates of State Activity in Product Liability Legislation. *Policy Studies Review* 10:61–78.

EPA (Environmental Protection Agency). 1985. *Guidance for Controlling Asbestos-Containing Material in Buildings*. Washington, DC: US Government Printing Office.

Epstein, Richard. 1988. The Political Economy of Product Liability Reform. *American Economic Review* 78, no. 2:311–15.

Esterling, Kevin. 2004. *The Political Economy of Expertise: Information and Efficiency in American National Politics*. Ann Arbor: University of Michigan Press.

Farhang, Sean. 2008. Public Regulation and Private Lawsuits in the American Separation of Powers System. *American Journal of Political Science* 52, no. 4:821–39.

———. 2010. *The Litigation State: Public Regulation and Private Lawsuits in the United States*. Princeton, NJ: Princeton University Press.

Feeley, Malcolm M., and Edward L. Rubin. 1998. *Judicial Policy-Making and the Modern State: How the Courts Reforms America's Prisons*. New York: Cambridge University Press.

Fiorina, Maurice. 1989. *Congress: Keystone of the American Establishment*. New Haven, CT: Yale University Press.

Fitzpatrick, Lawrence. 1990. The Center for Claims Resolution. *Law and Contemporary Problems* 53, no. 4:13–26.

Freeman, S. 2007. Deal Ends 6-Hour Strike at Chrysler; Automaker Say Union Trust to Run Retiree Health Care. *Washington Post*, October 11.

Frymer, Paul. 2003. Acting When Elected Officials Won't: Federal Courts and Civil Rights Enforcement in US Labor Relations, 1935–1985. *American Political Science Review* 97, no. 3:483–99.

George, Alexander, and Andrew Bennett. 2005. *Case Studies and Theory Development in the Social Sciences*. Cambridge, MA: MIT Press.

Gerring, John. 2004. What Is a Case Study and What Is It Good For? *American Political Science Review* 98, no. 2:341–54.

————. 2007. *Case Study Research: Principles and Practices.* New York: Cambridge University Press.

Gifford, Donald G. 2010. *Suing the Tobacco and Lead Pigment Industries: Government Litigation as a Public Health Prescription.* Ann Arbor: University of Michigan Press.

Glass, Robert P. 1983. The Asbestos Tragedy: Legal Issues and the Need for Reform. *University of Dayton Law Review* 8, no. 2:353–63.

Graber, Mark. 1993. The Nonmajoritarian Difficulty: Legislative Deference to the Judiciary. *Studies in American Political Development* 7:35–73.

Groseclose, Tim, Steven D. Levitt, and James M. Snyder Jr. 1999. Comparing Interest Group Scores across Time and Chambers. *American Political Science Review* 93:33–50.

Hacker, Jacob. 2002. *The Divided Welfare State: The Battle of Public and Private Social Benefits in the United States.* New York: Cambridge University Press.

————. 2004. Privatizing Risk without Privatizing the Welfare State: The Hidden Politics of Social Retrenchment in the United States. *American Political Science Review* 98, no. 2:243–60.

Hanlon, Patrick M. 2006. An Elegy for the FAIR Act. *Connecticut Insurance Law Journal* 12:517–82.

Hanlon, Patrick, and Anne Smetak. 2007. Asbestos Changes. *New York University Annual Survey of American Law* 62:525–606.

Hausegger, Laurie, and Lawrence Baum. 1999. Inviting Congressional Action: A Study of Supreme Court Motivations in Statutory Interpretation. *American Journal of Political Science* 43:162–85.

Henderson, James A., Jr., and Theodore Eisenberg. 1990. The Quiet Revolution in Products Liability: An Empirical Study of Legal Change. *UCLA Law Review* 37:479–553.

Hensler, Deborah. 2001. The Role of Multi-Districting in Mass Tort Litigation: An Empirical Investigation. *Seton Hall Law Review* 31:883–906.

————. 2002. As Time Goes By: Asbestos Litigation after *Amchem* and *Ortiz. Texas Law Review* 80, no. 7:1899–1924.

Hensler, Deborah, Stephen Carroll, Michelle White, and Jennifer Gross. 2001. *Asbestos Litigation in the US: A New Look at an Old Issue.* Santa Monica, CA: RAND Institute for Civil Justice.

Hensler, Deborah, William L. F. Felstiner, Molly Selvin, and Patricia A. Ebener. 1985. *Asbestos in the Courts: The Challenge of Mass Toxic Torts.* Santa Monica, CA: RAND Institute for Civil Justice.

Hensler, Deborah, M. Susan Marquis, Allan F. Abrahamse, Sandra H. Berry, Patricia A. Ebener, Elizabeth G. Lewis, E. Allan Lind, Robert J. MacCoun, R. Willard, G. Manning, Jeanette A. Rogowski, and Mary E. Vaiana. 1991. *Compensation for Accidental Injuries in the United States.* Santa Monica, CA: RAND Institute for Civil Justice.

Hensler, Deborah, R. Nicholas, M. Pace, Bonita Dombey-Moore, Beth Giddens, Jennifer Gross, and Erik K. Moller. 2000. *Class Action Dilemmas; Pursuing Public Goals through Private Gain.* Santa Monica, CA: RAND Institute for Civil Justice.

Higgins, Sean. 2005. Senate Asbestos Bill Gains New Life with Provisions Aimed at Democrats; Asbestos Stocks Climb as Specter Sees Deal on Proposed Trust Fund. *Investor's Business Daily*, April 13.

House Subcommittee on Labor Standards. 1983. The Effect of Bankruptcy Cases of Several Asbestos Companies on the Compensation on Asbestos Victims. Hearing, 98th Cong., 1st Sess., February 10.

Huber, Peter. 1991. *Galileo's Revenge: Junk Science in the Courtroom.* New York: Basic Books.

Ignagni, Joseph, and James Meernik. 1994. Explaining Congressional Attempts to Reverse Supreme Court Decisions. *Political Research Quarterly* 47:353–71.

Inside OSHA. 2005. House Asbestos Bill Gains Support as Senate Compensation Trust Fund Bill in Limbo. July 11.

IOM (Institute of Medicine). 2006. *Asbestos: Selected Cancers (Consensus Report).* Washington, DC: Institute of Medicine.

Issacharoff, Samuel. 2002. "Shocked": Mass Torts and Aggregate Asbestos Litigation after *Amchem* and *Ortiz. Texas Law Review* 80:1925–41.

Jacobson, Gary C. 2007. *A Divider, Not a Uniter: George W. Bush and the American People.* New York: Pearson.

Judicial Conference Ad Hoc Committee. 1991. *Report of the Judicial Conference on Asbestos Litigation.* Washington, DC: US Government Printing Office.

Kagan, Robert A. 1994. Do Lawyers Cause Adversarial Legalism? A Preliminary Inquiry. *Law and Social Inquiry* 19:1–62.

———. 2001. *Adversarial Legalism: The American Way of Law.* Cambridge, MA: Harvard University Press.

Kagan, Robert A., and Lee Axelrad. 1994. *Regulatory Encounters: Multinational Corporations and American Adversarial Legalism.* Berkeley: University of California Press.

Kakalik, James S., Michael G. Shanley, William L. F. Felstiner, and Patricia A. Ebener. 1983. *Costs of Asbestos Litigation.* Santa Monica, CA: RAND Institute for Civil Justice.

Kane, Paul. 2009. House Votes to Rebuke Wilson for Interruption. *Washington Post*, September 16.

King, Neil, and Sharon Terley. 2009. GM Collapses into Government Arms. *Wall Street Journal*, June 2. www.wsj.com/article/NA_WSJ_PUB:SB124385428627671881.com.

Kirp, David. 1979. *Doing Good by Doing Little: Race and Schooling in Britain.* Berkeley: University of California Press.

Kittel, Bernard, and Hannes Winner. 2005. How Reliable Is Pooled Analysis in Political Economy: The Globalization–Welfare State Nexis Revisited. *European Journal of Political Research* 44:269–93.

REFERENCES

Kjaergaard, J. and M. Andersson. 2000. Incidence Rates of Malignant Mesothelioma in Denmark and Prediction on Future Number of Cases among Men. *Scandinavian Journal of Work and Environmental Health* 26, no. 2:112–17.

Knight, J. 2005. Asbestos Stocks Hostage to Fate of Legislation on Liability. *Washington Post*, July 25.

Koniak, Susan P. 1995. Feasting While the Widow Weeps: *Georgine v. Amchem Products, Inc. Cornell Law Review* 80:1045–1158.

Lang, Robert D. 1985. Danger in the Classroom: Asbestos in American Public Schools. *Columbia Journal of Environmental Law* 11:111.

Leone, Robert A. 1986. *Who Profits: Winners, Losers and Government Regulation.* New York: Basic Books.

Lijphart, Arendt. 1971. Comparative Politics and Comparative Method. *American Political Science Review* 65:682–93.

Lilienfeld, D. E., J. S. Mandel, P. Coin, and L. M. Schuman. 1988. Projections of Asbestos Related Diseases in the United States, 1985–2009. *British Journal of Industrial Medicine* 45:283–91.

Los Angeles Times. 2010. Fixing the Filibuster. June 18. www.latimes.com/news/opinion/editorials/la-ed-filibuster-20100618 ,0,7909300.st ory.

Lovell, George. 2003. *Legislative Deferrals: Statutory Ambiguity, Judicial Power, and American Democracy.* New York: Cambridge University Press.

Lundqvist, Lennart J. 1980. *The Hare and the Tortoise: Clean Air Policies in the United States and Sweden.* Ann Arbor: University of Michigan Press.

Magnani, C., A. Agudo, C. M. Gonzalez, A. Andrion, A. Celleja, E. Chellini, P. Delmasso, A. Escolar, S. Herindez, C. Iveldi, D. Mirabelli, J. Remirez, D. Turuguet, M. Usel, and B. Terracini. 2000. Multicentric Study on Malignant Pleural Mesothelioma and Non-Occupational Exposure to Asbestos. *British Journal of Cancer* 83:104–11.

Mahoney, James, and Kathleen Thelen, eds. 2010. *Explaining Institutional Change: Ambiguity, Agency and Power.* New York: Cambridge University Press.

Mather, Lynn. 1998. Theorizing about Trial Courts: Lawyers, Policymaking, and Tobacco Litigation. *Law and Social Inquiry* 23:897–936.

Mayhew, David. 1974. *Congress: The Electoral Connection.* New Haven, CT: Yale University Press.

———. 2005. *Divided We Govern: Party Control, Lawmaking and Investigations.* New Haven, CT: Yale University Press.

McGovern, Francis. 1989. Resolving Mature Mass Tort Litigation. *Boston Law Review* 69:659–94.

———. 2003. Asbestos Legislation II: Section 524(g) without Bankruptcy. *Pepperdine Law Review* 31:233–60.

Mealey's Litigation Report: Asbestos Bankruptcy. 2005. CRMC to Stop Accepting Reports Prepared by Silica MDL Doctors. E-Mail Bulletin, September 14.

Melnick, R. Shep. 1983. *Regulation and the Courts: The Case of the Clean Air Act.* Washington, DC: Brookings Institution Press.

———. 1994. *Between the Lines: Interpreting Welfare Rights*. Washington, DC: Brookings Institution Press.

———. 1998. Strange Bedfellows Make Normal Politics: An Essay. *Duke Environmental Law & Policy* 9:75–94.

———. 2004. Courts and Agencies. In *Making Policy, Making Law: An Interbranch Perspective*, edited by Mark Miller and Jeb Barnes. Washington, DC: Georgetown University Press.

Moe, Terry M. 1989. The Politics of the Bureaucratic State. In *Can the Government Govern?* edited by J. Chubb and P. Peterson. Washington, DC: Brookings Institution Press.

Morone, James A. 1990. *The Democratic Wish: Popular Participation and the Limits of American Government*. New Haven, CT: Yale University Press.

Nagareda, Richard A. 2007. *Mass Torts in an Age of Settlement*. Chicago: University of Chicago Press.

Nelson, John R., Jr. 1985. *Black Lung: A Study of Disability Compensation Policy Formation*. Chicago: School of Social Service, University of Chicago.

Neustadt, Richard E. 1990. *Presidential Power and the Modern Presidents: The Politics of Leadership from Roosevelt to Reagan*. New York: Free Press.

Nicholson, W. J., G. Perkel, and I. J. Selikoff. 1982. Occupational Exposure to Asbestos: Population at Risk and Projected Mortality 1980–2030. *American Journal of Industrial Medicine* 3:259–311.

Nonet, Philippe. 1969. *Administrative Justice*. New York: Sage.

NIOSH (National Institute for Occupational Safety and Health). 2003. *Work-Related Lung Disease Surveillance Report 2002*. Washington, DC: NIOSH.

———. 2008. *Asbestos Fibers and Other Elongated Mineral Particles: State of Science and Roadmap for Research*. Washington, DC: Centers for Disease Control and Prevention and National Institute for Occupational Safety and Health, US Department of Health and Human Services.

Oberlander, Jonathan. 2003a. *The Political Life of Medicare*. Chicago: University of Chicago Press.

———. 2003b. The Politics of Health Reform: Why Do Bad Things Happen to Good Plans? *Health Affairs Web Exclusive*, W3–391, August 27. http://content.healthaffairs.org/cgi/reprint/hlthaff.w3.391v1.

Occupational Health Hazards Compensation Act of 1982 Hearings. 1982. 97th Cong., 2nd Sess., April 21.

O'Connell, Jeffrey. 1979. *The Lawsuit Lottery: Only the Lawyers Win*. New York: Free Press.

Office of Workers' Compensation. 2001. *Black Lung Benefits Act: Annual Report on the Administration of the Act*. Washington, DC: US Government Printing Office.

———. 2007. *Black Lung Benefits Act: Annual Report on the Administration of the Act*. Washington, DC: US Government Printing Office.

Orndorff, Mary. 2005. Ad Targets Sessions on Asbestos. *Birmingham News*, June 3.

Orren, Karen, and Stephen Skowronek. 2004. *The Search for American Political Development*. New York: Cambridge University Press.

Pan, Xue-lei, Howard W. Day, Wei Wang, Laurel A. Beckett, and Mark B. Schenkar. 2005. Residential Proximity to Naturally Occurring Asbestos and Mesothelioma Cases in California. *American Journal of Respiratory and Critical Care Medicine* 172, no. 8:1019–25.

Patashnik, Eric. 2000. *Putting Trust in the US Budget: Trust Funds and the Politics of Trust.* New York: Cambridge University Press.

Peacock, Andrea. 2003. *Libby, Montana: Asbestos and the Deadly Silence of an American Corporation.* Boulder, CO: Johnson.

Perine, Keith. 2004. No-Fault Asbestos Claims Fund Is a "Personal Priority" for Frist, but Cost Remains a Big Unknown. *CQ Weekly,* April 10, 865.

Peterson, Mark A. 1990. Giving Money Away: Comparative Comments on Claims Resolution Facilities. *Law and Contemporary Problems* 54, no. 4:113–36.

Peto, J., A. Deccarli, C. La Vecchia, F. Levi, and E. Negri. 1999. The European Mesothelioma Epidemic. *British Journal of Cancer* 79:666–72.

Pierson, Paul. 1994. *Dismantling the Welfare State: Reagan, Thatcher and the Politics of Retrenchment.* New York: Cambridge University Press.

———. 2004. *Politics in Time: History, Institutions, and Social Analysis.* Princeton, NJ: Princeton University Press.

Poole, Keith, and Howard Rosenthal. 2007. *Ideology & Congress*, 2nd ed. New Brunswick, NJ: Transaction.

PR Newswire. 2005. NPLC Applauds Senate Judiciary Committee for Passage of Asbestos Trust Fund Legislation. March 27.

Puzzanghera, John. 2009. Reform Plan Is Likely to Get a Rewrite. *Los Angeles Times,* September 24.

Rabkin, Jeremy. 1989. *Judicial Compulsions: How Public Law Distorts Public Policy.* New York: Basic Books.

Ragin, Charles. 2000. *Fuzzy Set Social Science.* Chicago: University of Chicago Press.

Rasmussen Reports. 2009. Voters Continue to See Deficit Reduction as Top Priority. November 20. Available at www.rasmussenreports.com/public_content/politics.

———. 2010. Budget Priorities. March 18. Available at www.rasmussenreports .com/public_content/politics.

Roberts, Jason M., and Steven Smith. 2003. Procedural Contexts, Party Strategy and Conditional Party Voting in the US House of Representatives, 1971–2000. *American Journal of Political Science* 47:305–19.

Rohde, David W. 1991. *Parties and Leaders in the Postreform House.* Chicago: University of Chicago Press.

Roggli, Victor L., Tim D. Oury, and Thomas A. Sporn, eds. 2004. *Pathology of Asbestos-Associated Diseases.* New York: Springer.

Schattschneider, E. E. 1935. *Politics, Pressure, and the Tariff.* New York: Prentice Hall.

Schickler, Eric. 2001. *Disjointed Pluralism: Institutional Innovation and the Development of the US Congress.* Princeton, NJ: Princeton University Press.

Schneider, Aaron, and David McCumber. 2004. *An Air That Kills: How the Poisoning of Libby, Montana Uncovered a National Scandal.* New York: Putnam.

Schroeder, Elinor. 1986. Legislative and Judicial Responses to the Inadequacy of Compensation for Occupational Diseases. *Law & Contemporary Problems* 49:151–82.

Schuck, Peter. 1986. *Agent Orange on Trial: Mass Toxic Disaster in Courts.* Cambridge, MA: Belknap Press.

———. 1992. The Worst Should Go First: Deferral Registries in Asbestos Litigation. *Judicature* 75:1–13.

Schwartz, Gary T. 1992. The Beginning and Possible End of the Rise of Modern Tort Law. *Georgia Law Review* 26:601–702.

Schwartz, Victor E., Mark A. Behrens, and Richard Tedesco. 2003. Congress Should Act to Resolve the National Asbestos Crisis: The Basis in Law and Public Policy for Meaningful Progress. *South Texas Law Review* 44:839–82.

Scott, W. Richard. 2008. *Institutions and Organizations: Ideas and Interests.* Los Angeles: Sage.

Selikoff, I., J. Churg, and E. C. Hammond. 1965. The Occurrence of Asbestos among Insulation Workers in the United States. *Annals of the New York Academy of Science* 32:139–55.

Shapiro, Martin. 1964. *Law and Politics in the Supreme Court: New Approaches to Political Jurisprudence.* New York: Free Press.

———. 1968. *The Supreme Court and Administrative Agencies.* New York: Free Press.

———. 1981. *Courts: A Comparative and Political Analysis.* Chicago: University of Chicago Press.

Silverstein, Gordon. 2009. *Laws Allure: How Law Shapes, Constrains, Saves, and Kills Politics.* New York: Cambridge University Press.

Sinclair, Barbara. 2000a. Hostile Partners: The President, Congress, and Lawmaking in the Partisan 1990s. In *Polarized Politics: Congress and the President in a Partisan Era,* edited by Jon R. Bond and Richard Fleisher. Washington, DC: CQ Press.

———. 2000b. *Unorthodox Lawmaking: New Legislative Processes in the US Congress,* 2nd ed. Washington, DC: CQ Press.

Skocpol, Theda, and Margaret Somers. 1980. The Uses of Comparative History in Macrosocial Inquiry. *Comparative Studies in Society and History* 12:174–97.

Smith, Barbara Ellen. 1987. *Digging Our Own Graves: Coal Miners and the Struggle over Black Lung Disease.* Philadelphia: Temple University Press.

Steinmo, Sven. 1994. American Exceptionalism Reconsidered: Culture or Institutions. In *The Dynamics of American Politics: Approaches and Interpretation,* edited by Lawrence Dodd and Calvin Jillison. Boulder, CO: Westview Press.

Steinmo, Sven, and John Watts. 1995. It's the Institutions, Stupid! Why Comprehensive National Insurance Always Fails in America. *Journal of Health Politics, Policy and Law* 20:329–423.

Stern, Seth. 2004a. Aiming for the Fast Track on Asbestos Bill. *CQ Weekly,* December 11, 2934.

———. 2004b. Daschle Trust Fund Proposal Revives Asbestos Negotiations, but Passage Is Still a Long Way Off. *CQ Weekly,* July 3, 1630.

———. 2005. Asbestos Bill Takes Big Step in Senate. *CQ Weekly,* May 27, 1448.

————. 2006a. Asbestos Bill Set Back on Point of Order. *CQ Weekly*, February 21, 492.

————. 2006b. Difficult Sticking Points on Asbestos. *CQ Weekly*, February 13, 4.

Stewart, Richard B., and Cass Sunstein. 1982. Public Programs and Private Rights. *Harvard Law Review* 95:1193–1322.

Stigler, George. 1971. The Theory of Economic Regulation. *Bell Journal of Economics and Management Science* 2:3–21.

Stiglitz, Joseph, Jonathan M. Orzag, and Peter R. Orzag. 2002. *The Impact of Asbestos Liabilities on Workers in Bankruptcy Firms*. New York: Sebago Associates.

Streeck, Wolfgang, and Kathleen Thelen. 2005. Introduction: Institutional Change in Advanced Political Economies. In *Beyond Continuity*, edited by William Streeck and Kathleen Thelen. New York: Oxford University Press.

Sugarman, Steven. D. 1989. *Doing Away with Personal Injury Law: New Compensation Mechanisms for Victims, Consumers, and Business*. New York: Quorum Books.

Teff, Harvey. 1985. Drug Approval in England and the United States. *American Journal of Comparative Law* 33:567.

Thelen, Kathleen. 2003. How Institutions Evolve: Insights from Comparative Historical Research. In *Comparative Historical Analysis in the Social Sciences*, edited by James Mahoney and Dietrich Rueschemeyer. New York: Cambridge University Press.

Tollison, Robert D. 1982. Rent Seeking: A Survey. *Kylos* 35:575–602.

Tweedale, Geoffrey. 2000. *Magic Mineral to Killer Dust: Turner & Newall and the Asbestos Hazard*. New York: Oxford University Press.

Tyler, Tom. 1990. *Why People Obey the Law*. New Haven, CT: Yale University Press.

Ursin, Edmund. 1981. Judicial Creativity and Tort Law. *George Washington Law Review* 49:229.

US House of Representatives. 1986. *Asbestos Hazard Emergency Response Act of 1986*. HR Rep. No. 763, 99th Cong., 2nd Sess. 14. Washington, DC: US Government Printing Office.

Vairo, Georgene. 2004. Mass Tort Bankruptcies: The Who, the Why, and the How. *American Bankruptcy Law Journal* 78:93–149.

Vinke, Harriet, and Ton Wilthagen. 1992. *The Non-mobilization of Law by Asbestos Victims in the Netherlands: Social Insurance versus Tort-Based Compensation*. Amsterdam: Hugo Sinzheimer Institute, University of Amsterdam.

Virta, Robert. 2003. *Worldwide Asbestos Supply and Consumption Trends from 1900 to 2000*. Washington, DC: US Geological Survey.

Walker, Alexander M., Jeanne E. Loughlin, Emily R. Friedlander, Kenneth J. Rothman, and Nancy A. Dreyer. 1983. Projections of Asbestos-Related Diseases. *Journal of Occupational Medicine* 25:409–25.

Weiler, Paul C. 1991. *Medical Malpractice on Trial*. Cambridge, MA: Harvard University Press.

Weiler, Paul C., Howard Hiatt, Joseph P. Newhouse, William G. Johnson, Troyen Brennan, and Lucian Leape. 1993. *A Measure of Malpractice: Medical Injury, Malpractice Litigation, and Patent Compensation*. Cambridge, MA: Harvard University Press.

Weir, Margaret. 1992. Ideas and the Politics of Bounded Innovation. In *Structuring Politics: Historical Institutionalism in Comparative Analysis*, edited by Sven Steinmo, Kathleen Thelen, and Frank Longstreth. New York: Cambridge University Press.

White House. 2005. UAW Endorses Specter Asbestos Draft Bill. Press Bulletin, April 14.

White, Michelle J. 2002. Why the Asbestos Genie Won't Stay in the Bankruptcy Bottle. *University of Cincinnati Law Review* 70:1319–40.

———. 2004. Asbestos and the Future of Mass Torts. *Journal of Economic Perspectives* 18:183–204.

Wilson, James Q. 1989. *Bureaucracy: What Government Agencies Do and Why They Do It*. New York: Basic Books.

Winship, Christopher, and Michael Sobel. 2004. Causal Inference in Sociological Studies. In *Handbook of Data Analysis*, edited by Alan Hardy and Melissa Bryman. London: Sage.

World Health Organization. 2006. Elimination of Asbestos-Related Diseases. Geneva: World Health Organization.

Young, J. T. 2006. A New Pattern of Partisan Balance Is Emerging. Scripps Howard News Service, December 16.

LEGAL CASES

Amchem Products, Inc., et al. v. George Windsor et al., 521 US 591, 716 (1997).

Beshada v. Johns-Mansville Products Corp., 90 N.J. 191 (N.J. 1983).

Borel v. Fibreboard Paper Products Corporation, 493 F.2d 1076 (5th Cir. 1973) rehearing and rehearing en banc denied, 493 F.2d at 1109, certiorari denied, 419 US 869 (1974).

CSX Transportation, Inc. v. Williams, 608 S.E. 2d 208 (Ga. 2005).

Daubert v. Merrell Dow Pharmaceuticals, Inc., 509 US 579 (1993).

Elmore v. Owens-Illinois, Inc., 673 S.W. 2d 434 (Mo. Sup. Crt. 1984).

Hardy v. Johns-Manville Sales Corporation, 681 F.2d 334 (5th Cir. 1982).

Holdampf v. A.C. & S., Inc. (In the Matter of New York City Asbestos Litigation), 5 N.Y. 3d 486 (Court of Appeals of New York, 2005).

INA v. Forty-Eight Insulation, Inc., 633 F.2d 1212 (6th Cir. 1980).

In re Asbestos and Asbestos Material Products Liability Litigation, 431 F.Supp. 906 (JPML 1977).

In re Report of the Advisory Group, 1993 WL 30497 (D. Me. Feb. 1, 1993).

In re USG Corp., 290 B.R. 223 (Bankr. D. Del. 2003).

Karjala v. Johns-Manville Products Corporation, 523 F.2d 155 (8th Cir. 1975).

Keene Corp. v. INA, 667 F.2d 1034 (1981).

Moran v. Johns-Manville Sales Corporation, 691 F.2d 811 (6th Cir. 1982).

Norfolk & Western Railway Co. v. Ayers, 538 US 135 (2003).

Olivio v. Owens-Illinois, Inc., 895 A. 2d 1143 (N.J. 2006).

Ortiz et al. v. Fibreboard et al., 527 US 815 (1999).

Sophia v. Owens-Corning Fiberglass, 601 N.W. 2d 627 (Wis. 1999).

INDEX

The letter *f* following a page number denotes a figure.
The letter *t* following a page number denotes a table.